HOW TO LOOK AT
OLD CHURCHES

HOW TO LOOK AT OLD CHURCHES

BY

H. SPENCER STOWELL

LATE ARCHÆOLOGICAL RECORDER, LONDON NATURAL
HISTORY SOCIETY

WEST END, STEWKLEY, BUCKS

FIFTH EDITION

METHUEN & CO. LTD.
36 ESSEX STREET W.C.
LONDON

First Published . . . February 26th 1925
Second Edition, Revised February   1926
Third Edition . . . June   1934
Fourth Edition . . . August   1945
Fifth Edition . . .   1946

CATALOGUE No. 3423/U

FOREWORD

THE author of this book, which in some ways is alone of its type in spite of the many volumes large and small dealing with the subject, has approached his task on first principles in trying to enter into the views and to satisfy the needs of the ordinary "man in the street" who desires to make a more intelligent study of England's old parish churches. His style is chatty and thus attractive even to a casual reader, and is consistently free from even simple technicalities, except those which he explains as he goes along for the guidance of the reader. These definitions, which he has kept down to a minimum, are quite original and very lucid, and their very ingenuousness of effect proves the ingenuity expended on their preparation. The sketches, too, are taken direct from churches visited by the author, and are therefore mostly fresh subjects, but have been kept as simple as possible so as first and foremost to illustrate the points which they are selected to elucidate. The pictorial draughtsmanship and advanced scholarship suitable for a larger work have been purposely subordinated—the whole scheme in fact is intended to suggest rather than to satisfy, and for this very reason the book should appeal to a wide range of the intelligent public, few of whom have not felt the fascination of these noble and romantic buildings, and this little book should be the solution to their problem. Moreover, I would urge that the younger generation should be more systematically taught in all our schools the study of old buildings, especially as graphic illustrations of the story of England's past.   To these also I would commend this simply-worded volume as their manual *par excellence*.   On the other hand, the book is not of the scattered and unconvincing nature of some small works of the kind, and does offer the more serious student a systematic though elementary foundation for further study.   Controversial subjects have been only tentatively treated.

Finally, it should stimulate the study not only of the architecture of mediaeval churches in this country but of the architecture of the past in every land.

H. V. MOLESWORTH ROBERTS

(UNIV. OF LOND. DIPLOMA IN ART
AND GILCHRIST MEDALLIST.)

WALLINGTON
July 1924

PREFACE

THIS little book is intended for those who have no knowledge of Architecture, but are pleased and interested, without knowing exactly why, when they find themselves in an old church, and feel that a greater interest would be well worth their while if only they knew how to proceed.

It may also help to cultivate the enthusiasm of those who, having already advanced beyond the initial step, wish to take a more intelligent interest in the subject.

Books on old churches are legion, but none is sufficiently simple to meet the needs of the beginner. For a true insight, however, into this fascinating subject, books are at best mere aids. The buildings themselves must be studied, if such a task of pleasure may be termed study. At first sight this may suggest insuperable difficulties to you, but a little considera-tion will show you that these are more apparent than real.

There is an old church in practically every village, town, and city throughout the land. There are others within easy walking or cycling distance, and many more in the scope of an afternoon's motor run, and they are of infinite variety in age and type.

I suggest that you spend an occasional hour looking round your parish church, which probably is always open. You will find that interest comes easily, and that you will not be content with the knowledge of one church but will go on to others, and make comparison between them. If you happen to live in a modernized suburb, the church in your immediate neighbourhood may have been rebuilt in modern times, but you will never need to go far afield for a really old one. Again, when you go for a holiday you will pass into a new district, where there will be a whole fresh series of churches, each with its own special features, awaiting your attention. In time you will probably arrange your holidays in such a way that you will gradually be able to visit churches in all parts of the country.

In this the following elementary notes will help you. I have dealt with general characteristics only, and have told the tale simply. I have been careful to omit all abstruse technicalities. They are quite unnecessary to the beginner, who will, without them, find himself speedily gripped by the fascination of the subject.

I make no pretence to lay before you the whole story of architecture. That, as I have said, is done in other more ambitious works. As my purpose is to introduce you to the subject, and to arouse your interest in it, I have confined my notes within reasonable limits. There is just sufficient matter to give you a very tolerable insight into one big phase, namely, our Church Architecture, not in ancient or modern times, but in the Middle Ages—in other words, GOTHIC ARCHITECTURE.

Throughout the history of the world man has produced a wonderful variety of Architectural Styles, but none is more interesting, none more easily understood, and none with more examples at hand, than this Gothic phase, which was fashioned here and on the Continent in mediaeval times.

The one other outstanding architectural production of civilization was known as Classic—originally in

vogue before the Gothic period—which was reintro-
duced at the end of the Middle Ages as a potent rival.
It was the Classic revivalists of that time who, in
their prejudice, gave the epithet "Gothic" to the
mediaeval style.

The Gothic style of the mediaeval period was preceded by the Saxon and Norman styles, as I shall
presently show you, and is confined, roughly speaking,
to the thirteenth, fourteenth, and fifteenth centuries.
More accurately, it began about the year 1150,
reached its zenith about 1275, and then declined,
till about 1475 it began to give place to the Tudor
style.

Photography and sketching will both be useful to
you. For instance, when photographing interiors of
buildings, a long exposure is required, and I suggest
that while the camera is silently doing its work you
make notes and sketches of anything particularly
interesting and not easy to photograph. Do not
think that you cannot sketch or draw, because
everybody can to a greater or lesser degree, and you
will find that in the actual effort of sketching you
will notice things you would otherwise miss, and a
greater impression of these details will be made on
your mind. Photography is perhaps more correct,
and a better record, but you will never regret making
your collection of sketches and notes.

For example, you will see, perhaps, an odd door in
a curious position and make a sketch of it because
you consider it is unique. Later on, after you have
visited a number of other churches many miles away
you will come across another such example in possibly
the same relative position.

Many such reasons for sketching will occur to you
when reading these notes, and afterwards in looking
at the churches, and, if you adopt my suggestion, a

valuable collection of original data will soon be in your possession.

I may say that I have aimed at first hand information throughout, having visited nearly every church I illustrate and many more besides, and my sketches are direct from the actual buildings so as to put forward new examples not already familiar in other works.

H. Spencer Stowell

70 Victoria Street, S.W. 1
    July 1924

CONTENTS

INTRODUCTION

IF, when next visiting an old church—of course with a seeing eye—you simply ask yourself, "Is the upper part of that window round, sharply pointed, or blunt pointed?" then you have plunged right into your subject. You can now date that window within a century or so. You proceed to try another window in the same church, and you will probably

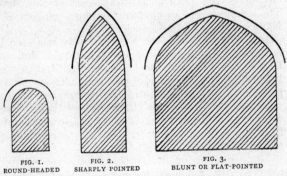

FIG. 1.
ROUND-HEADED

FIG. 2.
SHARPLY POINTED

FIG. 3.
BLUNT OR FLAT-POINTED

find that it is a hundred years earlier or later. And gradually the history of the church and the history of the people who worshipped there will be made clear to you. Architecture has well been described as the printing press of all ages.

The astounding thing is that it does not matter whether you are in Cornwall or Cumberland, in Kent or Carnarvon, the same characteristics with small local differences give you somewhere about the same date.

I write here of churches, but all my remarks apply equally to cathedrals, for the latter are but large, fully developed churches.

Whether the church is large or small, we shall find that the main part of it has one at least smaller part, as it were, growing out of it, something more than the Tower or Porch. If we enter the church we shall see why.

First, there will be the main large portion, which is called the Nave, and always leading out of the Nave towards the *East* is a part nearly always smaller called the Chancel. It does not matter where your church is, the Chancel is always east of the Nave. The simplest type of church, therefore, consists of a Nave leading on to a Chancel.

In mediaeval times the Nave not only was used to accommodate the worshippers at services, but was largely governed by the parishioners and served besides for non-religious purposes. There would probably be no other central gathering place for the villagers. It would be their village hall. They would also receive much of their religious teaching from the paintings which covered the walls, remains of which we shall look out for.

The Chancel, on the other hand, was entirely reserved for religious purposes, and only priest, servers, and singers had access. It was therefore more or less divided from the more secular Nave, but never completely separated from it, as the celebration in the Chancel was clearly followed by the congregation, and it was not at all irrational to connect life and religion together in this way in the one building.

The plan (Fig. 4) shows a small church with just a Nave and a Chancel. But the builders in earlier times had their problems of providing for an increased population, just as we have to-day. It is easy to see that the simplest way of increasing the accommodation of a building would be to cut arches through the side walls of the Nave and form Aisles, as they are

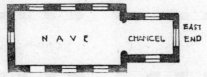

FIG. 4.   A SMALL CHURCH WITH NAVE AND CHANCEL

called, on the north and south sides of the church, as shown in the plan (Fig. 5). Such Aisles served also as processional paths.

A further way of enlarging the church was to widen only a part of the Nave, that end near the Chancel,

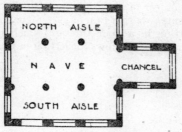

FIG. 5.   CHURCH WITH AISLES

which gives the form of a cross. These short arms of the cross are known as Transepts, and we shall find North Transepts and South Transepts, as shown in the plan (Fig. 6). Some will see here an interesting symbol of Christianity. Our airmen must often see this cruciform shape of churches as they look from above. They know that in all cases the one arm or head of the cross points east.

As the windows of a church give us a good insight

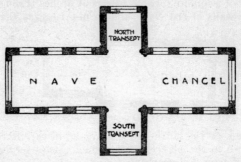

FIG. 6.   CHURCH WITH TRANSEPTS

into the dates of the various parts of a building, we shall later devote special attention to their form. The first object of any building is to shelter us from the elements, whether rain or sun. The first problem after putting in a door through which to enter, is that of inserting windows for letting in the light.

HOW TO LOOK AT
OLD CHURCHES

CHAPTER I

THE STYLES AND PERIODS

BEFORE considering details, it may be as well to realize that these churches were originally built in one style and at one period, but were later on, from time to time, owing to decay, fire, or the increase of population, rebuilt or enlarged. This gives us a variety of forms in one church. The shapes of the windows and other features and parts of the buildings show a great variation, and some of the forms or styles are simple, whilst others are elaborate. Thus at Worth Church in Sussex (Fig. 7), we look through a simple Saxon archway, and see in the distance an elaborate window. Both are in the same church, but were built at different times.

FIG. 7. AT WORTH, SUSSEX, WE LOOK THROUGH A SIMPLE ARCHWAY AND SEE IN THE DISTANCE AN ELABORATE WINDOW—BOTH IN THE SAME CHURCH, BUT BUILT AT DIFFERENT TIMES

The development from the early simplicity to the later elaboration came about in stages spread over some hundreds of years, but although the changes from one style to another were definite, their adoption was gradual. There was, of course, a certain amount of overlapping, as I shall later show. Because of this I shall touch upon the two styles which preceded and led up to the true Gothic.

It is necessary for convenience' sake to give each definite phase or style a name and I shall speak of, for example, the SAXON PERIOD and the NORMAN; then the TRANSITION and EARLY ENGLISH, the DECORATED and the PERPENDICULAR, which make up the Gothic Styles.

I shall refer to the Transition Norman simply as Transition.

The reasons for these particular names will be obvious later when we are considering the various characteristics of each style, for we shall find that the work of each Period possesses a distinctive style or form.

To make this clearer, I give on the opposite page a chart of the periods (Fig. 8). You will notice from this that each line representing the even hundred cuts through a style, as follows:

> 1000 cuts through SAXON.
> 1100 ,,   ,,   NORMAN.
> 1200 ,,   ,,   {TRANSITION and
>   {EARLY ENGLISH.}
> 1300 ,,   ,,   DECORATED.   }GOTHIC.
> 1400 ,,   ,,   PERPENDICULAR.   }

It may be said, therefore, that the styles are represented by the figures 10, 11, 12, 13, and 14.

Or it may be put this way: after the long Saxon period was expired,

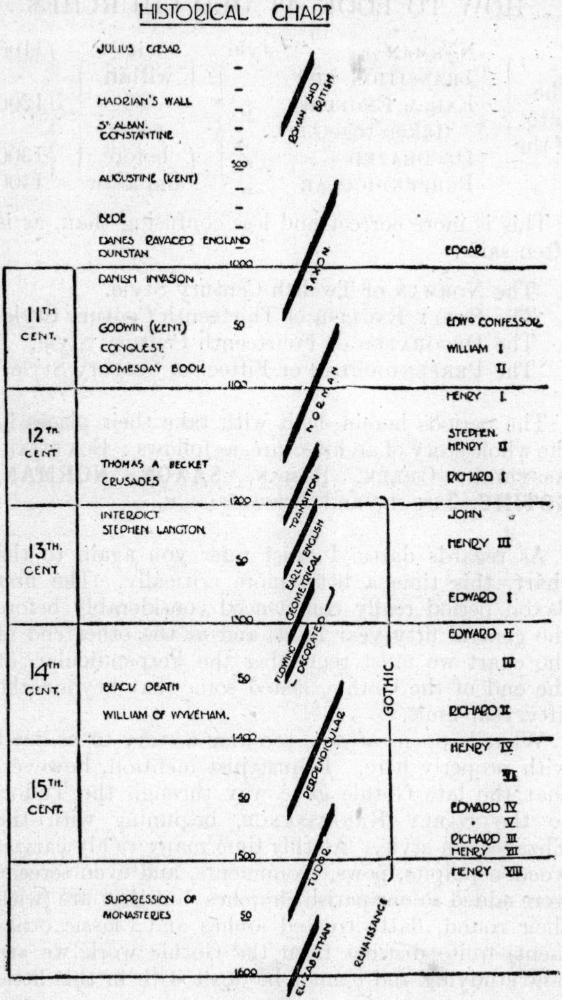

HISTORICAL CHART

JULIUS CÆSAR

HADRIAN'S WALL

S⁴ ALBAN.
CONSTANTINE

AUGUSTINE (KENT)

BEDE

DANES RAVAGED ENGLAND
DUNSTAN

DANISH INVASION

GODWIN (KENT)

CONQUEST

DOOMSDAY BOOK

THOMAS A BECKET

CRUSADES

INTERDICT
STEPHEN LANGTON

BLACK DEATH

WILLIAM OF WYKEHAM.

SUPPRESSION OF
MONASTERIES

11TH CENT.	50	EDGAR
		EDW⁴ CONFESSOR
	100	WILLIAM I
		II
12TH CENT.		HENRY I.
		STEPHEN.
		HENRY II
	1200	RICHARD I
13TH CENT.		JOHN
	50	HENRY III
	1300	EDWARD I
14TH CENT.	50	EDWARD II
		III
	1400	RICHARD II
15TH CENT.	50	HENRY IV
		VI
		EDWARD IV
	1500	RICHARD III
		HENRY VII
		HENRY VIII
	50	
	1600	

ROMAN AND BRITISH

SAXON

NORMAN

TRANSITION

EARLY ENGLISH
GEOMETRICAL

FLOWING
DECORATED

PERPENDICULAR

TUDOR

GOTHIC

RENAISSANCE

ELIZABETHAN

FIG. 8

	NORMAN style		1100
The	TRANSITION and	is	
date	EARLY ENGLISH „	within 50	1200
of the	(taken together)	years	
	DECORATED „	before	1300
	PERPENDICULAR „	and after	1400

This is more correct and less confusing than, as is often said :

The NORMAN or Twelfth Century Style.
The EARLY ENGLISH or Thirteenth Century Style.
The DECORATED or Fourteenth Century Style.
The PERPENDICULAR or Fifteenth Century Style.

The periods herein dealt with take their places in the whole story of architecture, as follows : EGYPTIAN, ASSYRIAN, GREEK, ROMAN, **SAXON, NORMAN, GOTHIC,** TUDOR, and RENAISSANCE.

As regards dates, I must refer you again to the chart, this time a little more critically. The first Saxon period really commenced considerably before the general fifty year limit, and at the other end of the chart we must remember the Perpendicular, at the end of the Gothic, lasted somewhat beyond the fifty year limit.

What happens after is too long a story to be dealt with properly here. I must just mention, however, that the late Gothic gave way through the Tudor, to the EARLY RENAISSANCE, beginning with the Elizabethan style. At this time many richly carved wooden pulpits, pews, monuments, and even screens were added to our parish churches, but they are (with their round, flatly treated arches and Classic ornament) quite distinct from the Gothic work we are now studying and cannot be dealt with in this little volume. The Renaissance was the result of a wave of reversion to old Greek and Roman Classic types. Up and down the country, particularly in large towns and cities, we have numerous examples of the fully developed Renaissance. In London the old Gothic churches which were destroyed in the Great Fire of London were rebuilt in this new fashion, many of them to the designs of that great architect Sir Christopher Wren.

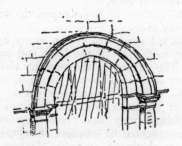

FIG. 8A. A TYPICAL RENAISSANCE DOOR

CHAPTER II

SAXON (ABOUT 600–1050)

I WILL now deal with the period which covers the time between the departure of the Romans in the year 407 and the Conquest of England by William the Conqueror in 1066.

It is the earliest of the six periods which go to make up my story.

You will not expect to find as many examples of it existing to-day as of the later and more recent periods. The extent of the remains visible to-day depends not so much on how active in church building the people were in a particular period as on the duration of time, between then and now, in which those buildings may have been impaired by the elements, plundered by enemies, or ravaged by fire.

There are, however, in spite of these agents of destruction, many interesting Saxon remains to be found in almost every county.

I will give some of the chief characteristics by which we may recognize the work of this period ; but what I show here only applies to late Saxon, for the primitive and rare remains of the earlier part of this period are not sufficiently important to be included in this limited survey. In other words, when any or all of these characteristics are noted you can date the work somewhere between 900 and 1050.

WALLS.—The walls are built with fairly small stones, which are irregular in size and shape. There

6

is plenty of mortar around each stone as indicated in the sketch (Fig. 9). This mortar not only binds the stones together but fills up the uneven spaces between the irregular stones. If the wall has been plastered over and the stones and the mortar joints are thus hidden, it will be almost impossible to date the wall.

The corners of a wall or the edge of a doorway or window were, however, dealt with quite differently;

FIG. 9. SMALL STONES OF IRREGULAR SIZE WITH PLENTY OF MORTAR

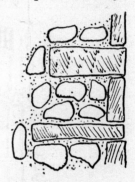

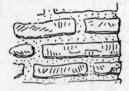

FIG. 9A. ROMAN BRICKS USED BY THE SAXONS

FIG. 10. THIS SAXON DOORWAY JAMB IS FROM BOSHAM, SUSSEX, AND SHOWS "LONG AND SHORT" WORK AT THE ANGLE OF A WALL BUILT OF SMALL IRREGULAR STONES WITH MUCH MORTAR BETWEEN THEM

there we shall note a long, thin stone placed *flat*, alternating with a long, thin stone placed in an *upright* position as shown at Bosham (Fig. 10).

If the corners of the wall were just treated with small stones they would soon break away or get knocked away; but the larger and heavier stones are more likely to remain in position, not only because of their extra weight, but also because they—especially the horizontal ones—are well tied into the wall; in fact, the horizontal stone goes through the thickness of the wall, as shown in the impost stone, Fig. 17, p. 14. Thus the horizontal stones enter into the formation of both corners of the side of the opening.

This arrangement is known as LONG and SHORT

FIG. 11.   EARLS BARTON

work, and is only found in buildings of the Saxon period.

These long and short stones were also at times arranged at intervals in the walls between the corners. The wall surfaces were thus given a panelled effect in some such way as shown at Earls Barton (Fig. 11).

I refer later, under Roman Influence, to the re-using of Roman tiles in Saxon walls.

It must be made quite clear that these features which we are considering are by no means found in all Saxon buildings ; some will be devoid of them, and the character and position of the masonry is our only guide.

PILASTER STRIP.—Another feature of Saxon walling, which may be found either by itself or in conjunction with the more elaborate features, is a small piece of walling which projects but a few inches from the main wall, at right angles to it. These strips are built on the long and short principle. It will be found that they are repeated at intervals, and the main wall is strengthened by their use.

Later on, as we note how all these features tend to develop into something more important, we shall find that this strip is made to project more than a few inches and will become worthy of the name " buttress," but in this

FIG. 12.
PILASTER STRIP, SOMPTING, SUSSEX

Saxon style the projection is nothing more than a strip (Fig. 12).

OPENINGS.—The openings in the outer walls for doorways and windows in churches of this period were small. For this there is a very good reason, and one which shows very clearly the relation between the lives of the people and the architecture they produced. The times were very unsettled, and individuals and communities were liable to attack at any time by robbers or invaders ; so every man, in addition to his ordinary avocation, had also to be a trained soldier, possessing arms and being skilled in their use for the defence of himself, his home, and his family. This fear of attack was so much a part of the lives of the people that it actually influenced the design of their churches, which were given small windows and narrow doors for defensive purposes. The doorways, moreover, were usually high in proportion to their width, which suggests that the men entered church carrying their weapons, probably staves or spears, or perhaps banners. The windows,

FIG. 13.
SAXON WINDOW SPLAYED INWARDS AND OUTWARDS

too, while they were always particularly small, were often still further reduced in the middle of the thickness of the wall, in the manner of loopholes, by their sides or jambs being "splayed" or built diagonally inwards and outwards. Thus the actual hole through which a marauder might try to enter was kept down to a minimum, but the approach to it, both from inside and outside, was enlarged by the splaying of the sides so as to admit the maximum amount of light (Fig. 13).

SEMICIRCULAR ARCH.—Most of these openings for the windows and doors were covered at the top with a round head, that is to say, the wall above the opening was carried, not by a flat stone right across the top, but by means of a half circle of small stones, or semicircular arch. In the larger arches, such as those found between the nave and chancel as at Bosham (Fig. 19), the shape may by no means be an exact semicircle; the outline often has a slightly uneven appearance, sometimes owing to the fact that the stonework has sunk, but it is practically semicircular in form.

Some of the windows were so small that it was not necessary to carry the wall over by means of an arch, and the top of the window could be covered merely by means of two stones slanting against each other and meeting at the top (Fig. 14). This type of window is known as *triangular headed*, and is rarely met with in subsequent styles. It is quite a strong arrangement, because over these narrow apertures there is not much weight to be carried.

FIG. 14. TRIANGULAR-HEADED WINDOW

TWIN WINDOWS.—Perhaps the most interesting Saxon window treatment was when two window openings were brought close together, side by side, and the little piece of wall in between was replaced by a small column, as shown at Bosham

FIG. 15. FRONT VIEW OR ELEVATION OF A TWO-LIGHT WINDOW FROM THE TOWER AT BOSHAM, SHOWING THE TYPICAL SAXON LONG AND SHORT WORK TOGETHER WITH A "MID-WALL" SHAFT

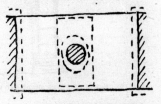

FIG. 15A. PLAN OF THE WINDOW SHOWN IN LAST SKETCH. DOTTED LINES INDICATE THE PROJECTING STONE ABACUS WHICH RESTS ON THE TOP OF THE COLUMN

(Fig. 15). This little column is not always as plain as here shown, for you will note that the other example given, at St. Albans, shows a column with rings around it (Fig. 16).

WOODEN CONSTRUCTION.—This latter design brings us to the consideration of wooden construction, because it shows that it is copied from a wooden prototype. The Early Saxons probably built mostly in wood and not in stone. A material like wood would evolve a certain design suited to that material, but the same design might well be copied in the other material. Let me make this quite clear. This example from St. Albans (Fig. 16), although it is in

FIG. 16. SAXON BALUSTER SHAFT AND ROMAN BRICKS RE-USED. ST. ALBANS

stone, looks as if it had been turned in a lathe, much as the legs of a table are turned at the present day. Again, the marble columns of the old Greek temples were probably copied in principle from the tree trunks which supported the roofs of the very early wooden temples. So we find that in some of the Saxon stone buildings certain forms and designs were used, which very strongly suggest that they were copied from earlier Saxon buildings of wooden construction.

A much greater area of the country in Saxon times was covered by forests than is the case to-day, and if stone were not available in the particular district in which a church was required, the builders would naturally choose timber as the building material. True, stone could be transported by horseback if the community who required a church happened to be near a Roman road, or the stone could be conveyed by water if they were near the sea-coast or a river ; but away from these facilities, and at the same time away from a stone district, they would have no alternative but to build with the timber found in the locality.

At Greenstead, near Chipping Ongar in Essex, there is a church portions of which retain to this day the original Saxon wooden walls, built like a log cabin, and it is truly remarkable that this woodwork should have lasted nearly a thousand years without falling from decay or having been destroyed by fire. From these remains we may see how the Saxons built in wood.

We can hardly expect to find many examples of Saxon construction in wood, for fire has destroyed many of them. Also we may bear in mind that these early Christian churches were built to symbolize Eternity, and their builders would naturally choose the best and most lasting materials available under the circumstances. Although timber is a very noble material with which to build a church—and if properly cared for is wonderfully lasting, as we have seen—it is not surprising to find that the Saxon examples handed down to us are in the more enduring material, stone.

MOULDINGS.—The Saxon stoneworker, then, took the rough stones from the quarry and roughly shaped them to suit the walls and fixed them together with mortar ; but when dealing with a doorway, for example, he would have to be more careful, as it was necessary for him to square up the stones in some way so as to form the sides of the doorway, and also

FIG. 17. SAXON DOORWAY, EARLS BARTON, NORTHANTS, SHOWING ROUND-HEADED OPENING WITH SLIGHTLY PROJECTING STRIPS. THE IMPOST STONES FROM WHICH THE ARCH SPRINGS ARE IN THIS CASE PLAIN AND NOT CARVED

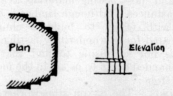

FIG. 18. RECESSED TREATMENT OF OPENING. FROM ST. ALBANS

it was necessary to shape the stones for the arch over, as we see from the example given from Earls Barton (Fig. 17).

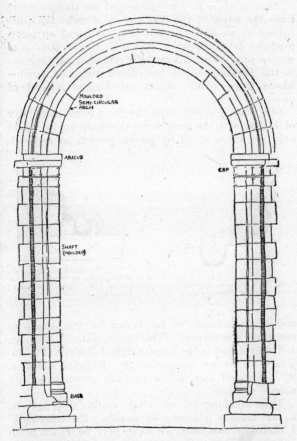

MOULDED
SEMI-CIRCULAR
ARCH

ABACUS

CAP

SHAFT
(MOULDED)

BASE

FIG. 19. CHANCEL ARCH AT BOSHAM, DIVIDING THE NAVE FROM THE CHANCEL. THE ARCH IS PRACTICALLY HALF ROUND IN FORM AND IS MOULDED WITH HOLLOWS, HALF ROUNDS AND SQUARE PORTIONS

After a while it was considered unsatisfactory to leave the edges of the doorways and archways quite square as at Earls Barton (Fig. 17), and an intermediate development is shown in the treatment of the opening at St. Albans (Fig. 18)—actually erected in the Norman period, but illustrating our point—where three small corners are formed instead of one.

Still, this was not quite the most convenient way of dealing with the corners, for the sharp angles would only get knocked off by people passing in and out,

FIG. 20. BOSHAM. CHANCEL ARCH: SECTION THROUGH ARCH

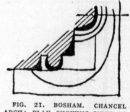

FIG. 21. BOSHAM. CHANCEL ARCH: PLAN SHOWING SIDES OR JAMBS OF THE OPENING, MOULDED

and it was considered far better for the mason to round off the corners. This last treatment is shown fully developed in the large sketch of Bosham (Fig. 19) where we find a comparatively elaborate example, with rounded and hollow portions alternating with square portions.

This breaking off of what would otherwise be square corners is known as *moulding* the stonework. I therefore say that we have here at Bosham an opening treated with a series of mouldings.

Mouldings, whether around doorways or windows, are extremely interesting and important, not only because of their variety, but for what they tell us in all the periods as to the date when they were executed.

HALF COLUMN.—Refer again to the Bosham sketches (Figs. 19, 20, 21, 22, and 24) and you will notice that in the large Chancel Arch the sides of the opening are moulded. The main outer moulding at the side is in reality a half column (Fig. 21).

The round arch over is also moulded (Fig. 20).

ABACUS.—We have seen that there is a square stone, not moulded, between the sides and the arch called the impost, from which the arch springs

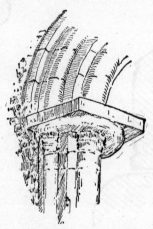

FIG. 22. BOSHAM. CHANCEL ARCH. THE MOULDED CAP WITH SQUARE ABACUS AND MOULDED ARCH ABOVE

(Figs. 19, 22, and 24). When this occurs at the top of a column it is also called the Abacus.

CAP.—The square abacus, together with the few horizontal mouldings immediately below it, are called the Capital, or Cap (Figs. 19, 22, and 24).

C

BASE.—At the bottom of the sides, and resting on the floor, are a few more horizontal mouldings and a square stone, which together are known as the base

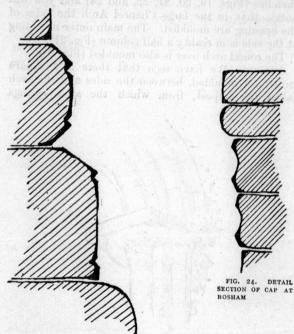

FIG. 24. DETAIL SECTION OF CAP AT BOSHAM

FIG. 23. DETAIL SECTION OF UPPER PART OF BASE AT BOSHAM

(Figs. 19, 21, and 23).   These stones are all characteristically very large.

ORNAMENT.—The sketch from Sompting (Fig. 25) shows a still further development.   An otherwise square stone, in this case a Cap, is carved in a primitive way in the form of some object, device, or symbol. Any such carving, which is different from a mere continuous moulding, must be referred to as *ornament*. This term, of course, applies to the carving of any device or design, more than a mere

FIG. 25. A CARVED SAXON CAP AT SOMPTING WHICH REMINDS
ONE OF THE CLASSIC VOLUTE OR SCROLL

moulding. The carved ornament in this style is somewhat rare and often crude, but always of great interest.

ROMAN INFLUENCE.—Just prior to this period this country had been under Roman influence—it was in fact a Roman province—and, although the last of the Roman leaders had taken their departure as early as the year 407, some hundreds of years before the time of the Saxon examples which we have been discussing, the Saxons would have a number of Roman buildings around them up and down the country.

The Romans had been sufficiently civilized to *create* a building material by baking clay—of which there was plenty at hand in this country—into bricks and tiles when timber and stone were not available. In fact, the Roman was quite capable of showing off his skill in baking bricks, even when other material was already in existence. The Saxons, on the other hand, were primitive and were quite prepared to re-use any sound material from a neighbouring ruin, and therefore frequently took Roman bricks and tiles from Roman ruins and re-used them. You will note Roman bricks in the arches over the Saxon columns at St. Albans (Fig. 16). As far as we know, they did not trouble to make bricks, even if they knew how. We do know, however, that they were strongly influenced by this Roman work, and they copied it to a certain extent; for the Romans built with columns and round arches, and the Saxon interpretation of this is found at Bosham (Fig. 19), with its half column and round arch. If you have studied Roman architecture you will note that there is a Roman "feeling" about the little piece of carving from Sompting (Fig. 25), and much other Saxon ornament. There was also indirect Roman influence from the Continent, where a modified Roman style was in vogue.

NORMAN INFLUENCE.—As it is important to note that the change from one style to another was always gradual, I must say a few words as to the extent to which the Saxons were influenced by their successors, the Normans.

At the end of this Saxon style, when the Roman influence had quite died out, we shall find that, although William the Norman did not come over and conquer this country until the year 1066, these islands were sufficiently near to Normandy to be influenced architecturally by the Norman style, which was already being developed on the Continent, and we shall note but little difference at first between the late Saxon style and the early Norman which succeeded it.

OVERLAPPING OF STYLES.—Whilst you are mastering the characteristic features of each style there will be just one note of warning to bear in mind, viz. that each style was liable to be carried over into the succeeding period. For example, when the Normans took possession of England there still remained many Saxon builders who would carry on in their own fashion, whilst the Normans were busy building elsewhere. The conquerors and the conquered may often have worked side by side, or the Saxons may have been told to build and were left to themselves to design and build after their own manner. This we see in several examples of late Saxon character built in the early Norman period.

It must also be pointed out that any change in style would take place earlier in the larger and more important churches than in the smaller churches of the villages. The style therefore developed more in some districts than in others according to the greater or lesser contact with the big cities, which would usually have the best craftsmanship and the most advanced thought.

SUMMARY

SAXON (600–1050)

Recognizable Features of 900–1050

1. WALLS.—Small and irregular-shaped stones for rough work. Very large squared stones for more important work. An arrangement of long and short stones at the corners and at intervals.

2. PILASTER STRIPS of slight width and projection.
3. WINDOWS.—Small, with double splay, inside and out; semicircular or triangular-headed arches. Double windows divided by baluster or small column. Small columns in imitation of " turned " wood.
4. DOORWAYS.—Small, high, and narrow, with semicircular arch.
5. MOULDINGS.—Bold. Half round and corresponding hollows.
6. ORNAMENT.—Crude, rare.
7. MATERIALS.—Stone, common. Wood, rare.
8. INFLUENCES.—Roman, direct or indirect. Norman.

CHAPTER III

NORMAN (ABOUT 1050-1160)

WHEN the Normans conquered England they brought along their own architectural style, just as the Romans had done theirs a thousand years before. The architecture of Normandy, although founded upon Roman principles of construction, was a distinct version of its own. You will find that some of the most interesting architectural remains in this country are of the Norman period, built not *in* the Roman manner, but *after* the Roman manner. The Roman style made use of large stones (or small bricks), whilst the Normans only used comparatively small stones and were not clever enough or did not trouble to bake bricks. The Normans used the Roman column, but usually on a small scale. From these beginnings they developed their own individual characteristics.

Although the Norman Conquest in 1066 brought about a great change in these islands, the early Norman builders built, particularly in the simpler examples, sufficiently like the Saxon to cause us sometimes to confuse the late Saxon with the early Norman, but you will find that the Normans soon developed features which, as I will show later, are different from the work of their predecessors.

We shall see an abundance of this work, for a great many examples of this style have been handed down. Occasionally you will only find one arched doorway or a window, possibly a series of arches or "arcade," or more rarely a whole building in this style. Many people once appear to have believed that the world would end in the year 1000; but after this date, as their fears had not been fulfilled, they immediately set about with feverish activity to build churches everywhere. They built thousands of churches during these one hundred years, and many of these, or parts of them, exist to this day. What shall we find characteristic of this Norman period?

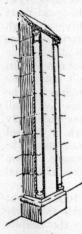

FIG. 26.
NORMAN BUTTRESS

WALLS.—Some of the early walling was of unevenly shaped stones, but often, particularly as the style advanced, the stones in the walls were shaped up into square forms. The more carefully the stones were squared the less mortar there was required, and the mortar joints, as they are called, therefore became thinner as time went on. Moreover, the walls were thicker than in Saxon times, and we do not meet with large stones going through the thickness of the wall.

BUTTRESSES.—In the Saxon style we noted that occasionally the walls were strengthened by little pilaster strips which projected out a few inches, at right angles to the wall, but in the Norman style these strips project much farther, and became what I must call, owing to their greater importance, Buttresses. The main structure was therefore strengthened by what were practically short pieces of wall projecting from the outside walls of the church. The early buttresses would have a less

projection than the later ones, and as the style
advanced the corners of the buttresses would have
their outer edges worked off into mouldings or little
columns as shown in Fig. 26.

OPENINGS.—All the arches were semicircular in
form. The windows were usually small, as we found
them in the Saxon period, and for the same protective
reason, for during the hundred years which we are
now considering there were insurrections, invasions,

FIG. 27. NORMAN
WINDOW WITH DEEP
SPLAY, WESTHAM, SUS-
SEX

FIG. 28. EAST END OF STEWKLEY. NORMANS WERE NOT
GIVEN TO GROUPING THEIR WINDOWS, BUT THEY SOME-
TIMES PUT A BLIND ARCH AT EACH SIDE OF A WINDOW

and civil wars; many a time the land would be in
turmoil, and each church would become a local
stronghold.

In the Saxon style the actual windows were in the
middle of the wall with a splay both inwards and
outwards (see Fig. 13), but in this Norman period it was
usual to put the actual window very near the outside
of the wall and have only one splay, on the inside.
The actual opening was in the earlier part of the
period extremely narrow, being often only a few
inches wide, as shown at Westham, Sussex (Fig. 27),

but later bigger and taller windows were erected (Fig. 28).

In the earlier days of this style the larger arches have plain square edges and are not moulded, but sometimes there is a moulding running round as an outer ring, which is known as a HOOD MOULD, as shown in Fig. 29.   Then, in the later work of this style we shall find that the opening is covered by an arch within an arch, receding one inside the other

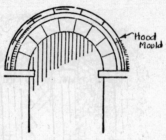

FIG. 29

like a nest of boxes.   This arrangement of a multiple arch not only occurs over the larger openings, but is very often found in the smaller round arches over the doorways, as at Burpham (Fig. 30), and sometimes around the windows.   Under these arches we shall find that the wall is cut away at the sides, forming small columns, a column more or less under each arch.

We may, then, say that these openings have recessed arches, with columns in the recessed sides or jambs of the openings.

COLUMNS.—Columns (I use this word throughout for the sake of uniformity and because it is generally understood) will be found supporting the chancel arch, the nave arches, or at the sides of doorways and windows. These have bases on the floor and caps at the top, as in all styles. The portion between the base and the cap is known as the shaft, and is usually, though not always, round. We cannot always tell the date of a shaft, for its shape too often varies.

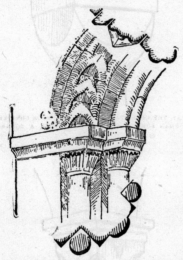

FIG. 30. A NORMAN DOORWAY FROM BURPHAM, SUSSEX. THE PLAN SHOWS COLUMNS AND HALF COLUMNS IN A JAMB OF THE DOORWAY. THE ARCH IS CHARACTERISTICALLY WORKED

CAPS.—The caps, however, are very distinctive in this period. The upper part of nearly all Norman caps is formed of a square stone, the abacus on which the arch immediately rests, as shown in Fig. 31.

The squareness of the abacus makes a good contrast to the curve of the arch above. It is such a contrast as this, together with the general harmony elsewhere, which gives the old churches such a pleasing and satisfactory appearance, for contrast and harmony are fundamentals in all the arts and are here just as necessary as in life itself.

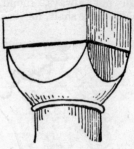

FIG. 31. A CAP, THE UPPER PART OF A COLUMN, FROM CHESTER CATHEDRAL. THIS EARLY NORMAN FORM IS A CUSHION CAP WITH A SQUARE ABACUS OR UPPER PART

FIG. 32. FROM THE TOWER OF LONDON, SHOWING A MOULDED ABACUS AND A MORE ELABORATE TREATMENT OF THE LOWER PART OF THE CAP

The lower part of the cap, beneath the abacus, is formed in various ways, as we see from the examples given (Figs. 31–33). In every case, however, the problem was the same, namely, to join the square abacus to the round shaft below. But the method of dealing with the problem is different in each case.

In the first of the three examples (Fig. 31) the part below the abacus and above the shaft resembles a cushion in form, and this cap is known as a Cushion Cap. Its date would probably be before 1100.

In the second example (Fig. 32) a square block is taken and the corners are shaped away as shown, whilst in the third (Fig. 33) the treatment used is known as Scalloping and the cap is called a Scalloped Cap. Its date would be after 1100.

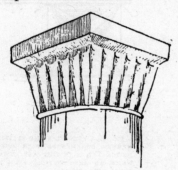

FIG. 33. A LATE NORMAN CAP FROM LOWER BEBINGTON, CHESHIRE, SHOWS A STILL FURTHER DEVELOPMENT, KNOWN AS A SCALLOPED CAP

I only give these three varieties. You will find other variations; but most of them will fall into, or approximate to, one or other of the three categories given.

The more elaborate cap did not appear before 1125.

MOULDINGS AND ORNAMENTS.—One of the chief charms of this style is its wealth of mouldings and ornament, and it is important to make the meaning of those terms quite clear.

In the first sketch (Fig. 34) the stone is square and neither moulded nor ornamental.

In the second sketch (Fig. 35) a continuous *moulding* is formed on or in the stone ; but in the sketch (Fig. 36) there is a device—one of a variety of forms —which is cut intermittently and not a continuous formation. This last is known as an *ornament*. Thus, referring back for a moment to the Burpham example (Fig. 30), the inner stones of the arch are moulded, the lower part of the abacus is " moulded," but the

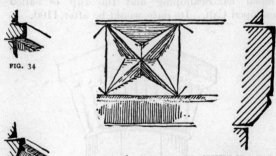

FIG. 34

FIG. 35

FIG. 36. ELEVATION AND SECTION OF A FLAT MEMBER ORNAMENTED WITH A NORMAN STAR DESIGN AND IS IN THIS CASE AN IMPOST (FROM WHICH AN ARCH SPRINGS) FROM THE CHANCEL ARCH, FORD, SUSSEX

cap itself and the middle part of the arch are " ornamented."

In subsequent styles a moulding was either left as such or an ornament was worked on or at the side of it ; but the unique thing about the work of the Norman builders was that they not only did this, but also sometimes broke the continuity of the line of the moulding itself, as shown in the example given from Tortington (Fig. 37). In this way the moulding itself became an ornament.

Some of the Norman churches are to-day very beautiful and full of harmony, and always the result is obtained by the simplest means.

The three simplest mouldings with which we are likely to meet in this style are :

SPLAY or CHAMFER, which is merely cutting off the
    stone at an angle (Fig. 38).
A ROUND (Fig. 39).
A HOLLOW (Fig. 40).

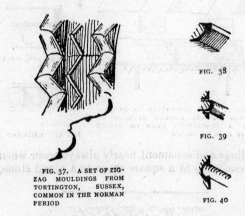

FIG. 37. A SET OF ZIG-ZAG MOULDINGS FROM TORTINGTON, SUSSEX, COMMON IN THE NORMAN PERIOD

FIG. 38

FIG. 39

FIG. 40

A QUIRK, a small acute incision used in conjunction
    with other and larger mouldings, as in Fig. 36,
    where the quirk appears immediately under the
    star pattern, and again immediately over the
    pellet in Fig. 43.

These may be found employed singly, but usually many of these mouldings run side by side, in conjunction with each other, as shown in Figs. 41–45.

There may be a carved representation of a bird's beak, or a form suggestive of a cat's head, overlapping a series of mouldings.

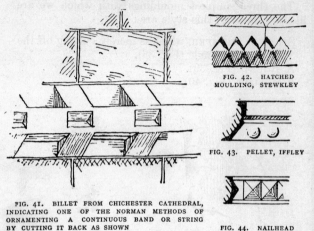

FIG. 42. HATCHED MOULDING, STEWKLEY

FIG. 43. PELLET, IFFLEY

FIG. 44. NAILHEAD

FIG. 41. BILLET FROM CHICHESTER CATHEDRAL, INDICATING ONE OF THE NORMAN METHODS OF ORNAMENTING A CONTINUOUS BAND OR STRING BY CUTTING IT BACK AS SHOWN

Mouldings and ornament nearly always occur when it is necessary to fit a square stone to a round stone,

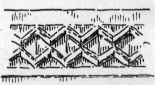

FIG. 45. A LOZENGE MOULDING AT STEWKLEY, BUCKS, RESULTING FROM TWO ZIGZAGS ARRANGED SIDE BY SIDE. DATE, 1150

or to ease off the squareness of a window for the purpose of letting in more light, or in the case of a doorway to make it easier to pass in or out.

An ornament, pure and simple, however, may be applied to broader surfaces, of which there are many. For instance, a doorway is usually round-headed, because it is easier to cover an opening by means of an arch of small stones than by one heavy flat stone, even if such were available ; yet the door itself is square, the simplest shape for a wood frame, thus leaving a half circle approximately filled in by a stone slab called a "Tympanum," like that at Stewkley

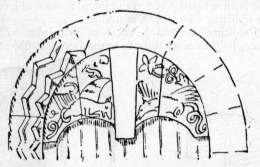

FIG. 46.   UPPER PART OF A NORMAN DOORWAY AT STEWKLEY.   DATE, 1150.
FILLED IN UNDER THE ARCH BY A CARVED " TYMPANUM "

(Fig. 46). It was usually carved, for this does not weaken the structure, and serves to portray some incident or some form of symbolic teaching.

PRINCIPLE OF ORNAMENT.—There is a reason for all the various forms which we meet with in architecture. No great building, no structure worthy of the adjective " beautiful," owes its quality to meaningless ornament or decoration *applied* or stuck on to make it so. It is beautiful only because every part and every feature which goes to make the whole is there for an honest and suitable purpose. Even in engineering, in which there is no pretension to

D

æsthetic qualities, an honestly designed locomotive may be, and often is, a thing of some beauty, but never can a railway bridge, or any other example, really please the eye which has had some superfluous ornament put on to it, " to try," as we say, " to make it look pretty," without a real purpose.

If this principle of honest design helps æsthetically in the realm of engineering, how much more is it necessary in architecture, which is not merely useful but is an art with the definite moral mission of having an uplifting effect upon mankind.

Realizing something of these principles will, I trust, help us more fully to appreciate our subject.

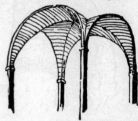

FIG. 47. BARREL VAULT

FIG. 48. INTERSECTING VAULTS WITH GROINS AT INTERSECTIONS

VAULTING AND THE POINTED ARCH.—I have said that the early Saxon buildings were often built of wood, and then later the change was made to a stone construction. After this change was made it is very probably true to say that the subsequent builders kept to wood as the medium in which to construct the roofs of their churches, and the early Normans probably did so too. Now, the later Normans considered it advisable to protect their wooden roofs against damage by fire, and this was done, in larger churches at any rate, by means of stone ceilings. These stone ceilings, or vaults, as we more correctly

name them, took the same form as the round arch, and
the result was a long tunnel or Barrel Vault (Fig. 47).

I may here note that the round arch and barrel
vault are both of very ancient origin, and I do not
for a moment suggest that either *originated* in this
period or even the Saxon.

It occurred sometimes that one of these tunnels
would have to run into another at right angles, and
so projecting edges or Groins would be formed at the

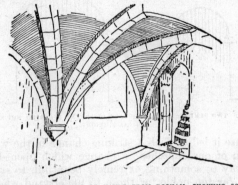

FIG. 49. A STONE CEILING OR VAULT FROM BOSHAM, SHOWING SQUARE
GROINED VAULTING

intersections, and we get as a result a GROINED
VAULT, as shown in Fig. 48.

These groins at the intersections of the vaulting
gradually developed into projecting VAULTING RIBS
and appear as a projecting framework of stone, and
we see this framework on looking up at the ceiling,
as sketched, at Bosham (Fig. 49).

We may therefore have, first, a single barrel vault ;
secondly, two such vaults intersecting forming pro-
jections called groins ; and thirdly, the projecting
groins appearing as stone ribs:

Till now I have always spoken of the openings as being covered by round, or, strictly speaking, half-round, arches, but later on, in subsequent styles, it will be a pointed arch which covers the openings.

This change was due to a curious problem which arose when the Normans worked out their stone vaulting, and I must lay some stress on this development not only because of its great interest, but

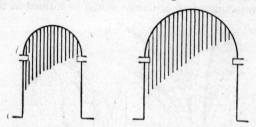

FIG. 50.   TWO SEMICIRCULAR ARCHES OF DIFFERENT SPANS DO NOT REACH
THE SAME HEIGHT

because it led to such a striking change in the whole design of our churches—a change which opened up the way to something extremely beautiful, to something far too noble for those to understand who do not to some extent have its mysteries explained.

Now, we shall speak of the distance between the supports of an arch or a vault as the SPAN.

If two half-round vaults cut into each other at right angles, and if these two vaults were of the *same span*, the tops of the vaults would then reach to the same height and everything would be quite straightforward (Fig. 48).

Now imagine two half-round vaults of *differing* spans (as at Fig. 50) cutting into each other, then the top of the narrower vault would not reach to the same height as the top of the wider vault.   To put it another way : two half-round arches of different spans will not reach to the same height (Fig. 50). In order to overcome this difficulty the Normans at first stilted the arch of the lesser span, i.e. raised it on straight pieces to make the top come to the same height as the wider arch. The arch started off with a straight upright piece before taking the curved form.

This arrangement was not for long considered to be a satisfactory one. It gave the impression that some mistake had occurred. We see the stilted arch sometimes, as shown in Fig. 51, but its form soon

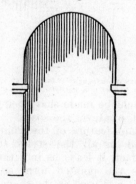

FIG. 51. STILTED ARCH

gave way to one which was much more satisfactory, namely, the Pointed Arch, which effectively solved the problem. I will show you how.

Return for a moment to the problem of the two arches of differing spans. If you deal with the one which has the lesser span by using a POINTED ARCH, then it will reach to the height of the other one (Fig. 52). The reason is that a round arch must reach to a certain height when the span is fixed, but a pointed arch is alterable to any height, quite apart from its span.

This was a simple solution when once thought of, and so, when the Pointed Arch was discovered, it was found that, whatever its span, it could be made to reach any desired height. All the problems of intersecting vaults of varying spans were solved by this *elastic form of the Pointed Arch*.

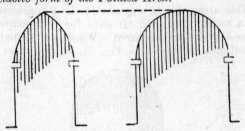

FIG. 52. TWO ARCHES OF DIFFERENT SPANS MAY BE MADE TO REACH THE SAME HEIGHT IF A POINTED ARCH IS USED

The arch could be made sharp-pointed, or blunt-pointed at will, whatever the span.

This important feature of the Pointed Arch was finally adopted in all the styles succeeding the Norman. In fact, it leads us into the true Gothic. Not only was the pointed form adopted in the vaulting, but it was used as the shape of the arches over the windows in the walls under the vault, and was eventually adopted for all the openings throughout the building, for doorways or windows or any of the arcading. But the change in the arch form from the round to the pointed was by no means sudden. It came about gradually, as did all the varying features of the different styles.

I have referred to this new form of arch here under the Norman style in order to preserve the continuity, because it was introduced at the end of the Norman

period. It was, however, so different from the
Norman round arch, and was accompanied by such
a marked tendency to the lighter and more graceful
character of the succeeding Early English style, that
it is expedient to emphasize, as a separate TRANSITION
period, this intervening phase, when Norman characteristics were dying out, and were giving way by
degrees to the birth of the true Gothic of lighter
construction and pointed arch, and yet the whole of
the old forms survived for a while side by side with
the youth of the new forms and graces ; for the death
of the one did not take place until the other had
become fairly well established.

SUMMARY

NORMAN (1050–1160)

1. WALLS.—Square stones with thick mortar joints
   (early) and thin joints (late).
2. BUTTRESSES.—Much deeper than the Saxon
   pilaster strip.   Corners sometimes moulded.
3. OPENINGS.—All arches half-round. Windows
   small. Internal splay, sometimes with recessed
   arches and columns in the recesses of the
   jambs. Doorways with recessed and moulded
   arches and columns in the recesses of the jambs.
4. COLUMNS.—With distinctive caps, such as
   Cushion and Scallop.
5. MOULDINGS.—Chamfer, round, hollow, quirk.
6. ORNAMENTS.—Zizgag, star, hatched, pellet, nailhead, lozenge, bird's beak.
7. VAULTING.—Projecting groins or ribs, sometimes
   unequal and variously treated by stilting, etc.,
   lead up to evolution of the pointed arch.

CHAPTER IV

TRANSITION (1160–1200)

IN dealing with this period of transition we shall find that the older and heavier Norman style, with its round arch, was still struggling for existence, side by side with the pointed arch, and both types occur together in the same building. As the latter form of arch has a more graceful and lighter appearance than its predecessor, so there is now a tendency to lighten the construction and the appearance of all the features of the churches.

The heavy masses of stonework were relieved by more carving than we noted in the Norman style, and the columns cut out from the projecting corners of the stonework in various parts of the church were greater in number but smaller. Above all, as the style proceeded the POINTED ARCH became predominant.

The stone ceiling or vaulting was often of pointed form, and the ribs at the intersections, instead of being somewhat clumsy, square, projecting stones, were carved or otherwise relieved by mouldings, with the result that heaviness gave place to a lightness and greater elegance, as shown later in the vaulting at Aldingbourne (Fig. 68, p. 50).

The large square piers or columns now have their corners formed into small columns (Fig. 54). Again, the small column in the recesses of the doorways, for example, was sometimes partly attached and was cut out of the same stones as the solid work behind, or it might be quite detached and of one tall stone, leaving a space behind the column.

The doorway and window openings were covered by either round arches or pointed ones, for this

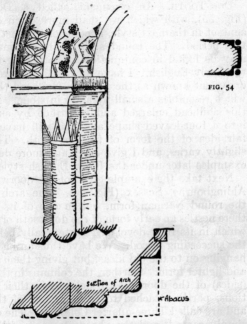

FIG. 54

Section of Arch

Abacus

FIG. 53.   TORTINGTON, SUSSEX.   LATE NORMAN OR TRANSITION
TREATMENT OF DOORWAY, c. 1250

Transition period gives us something of its predecessor and something of its successor; therefore, the round and the pointed characteristics are intermingled in a very interesting way.

The mouldings generally were more deeply cut and

closer together than in the Norman manner, and they therefore throw greater shadows and are in many ways more interesting and possess more character. The carving of the ornament was certainly more elaborate and began to follow plant types.

DOG-TOOTH.—An ornament called a Dog-tooth (Fig. 55), with which we shall more often come in contact in the next style, is occasionally met with in this period. The round arch of the Norman style may be found in conjunction with the dog-tooth of the Early English. I have previously referred to an ornament known as the Norman Nailhead (Fig. 44), which resembles a small pyramid in stone. Imagine this nailhead enlarged and beautified by cutting it into a four-leaved shape and you will have a very fair idea of the form of the dog-tooth. The form slightly varies, and I give other and more developed examples later under the Early English style.

Next take the example given of the doorway from Aldingbourne, Sussex (Fig. 56). The arch retains the round Norman form, but in one of its hollows there nestles an early form of the dog-tooth ornament, which in its fully developed state really belongs to the succeeding period. We have thus an instance of hanging on to the old ideas, but giving them a newer and lighter form. Further, the columns in the jambs (sides) of the doorway are delicate in their proportions, partly attached to the masonry of the wall, and are called Three-quarter Columns. The caps are simply carved, and the abacus treated with a bold round moulding ; finally, the bases show slight but certain signs of improved character.

It is interesting to follow the development of another Norman feature, namely, the Norman Cushion Cap. It is now fully carved, the old rounded portions are now hollowed away to form a " bell "

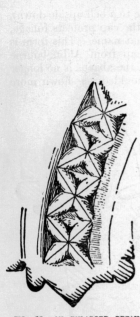

FIG. 55. AN ENLARGED DETAIL SECTION AND ELEVATION OF THE DOG-TOOTH ORNAMENT WHICH IS OCCASIONALLY MET WITH IN THIS TRANSITION PERIOD BUT REALLY BELONGS TO THE SUCCEEDING EARLY ENGLISH PERIOD

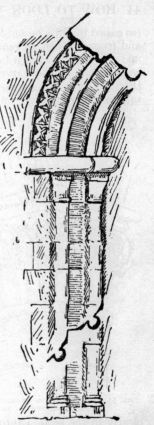

FIG. 56. A TRANSITION DOORWAY FROM ALDINGBOURNE, SUSSEX. THE ROUND ARCH OF THE NORMANS IS RETAINED BUT THE MOULDINGS ARE MORE DEEPLY CUT, AND ONE OF THEM IS ENRICHED WITH THE DOG-TOOTH ORNAMENT. THERE ARE SMALL COLUMNS IN THE JAMBS. DATE, c. 1190.

(so called from its resemblance to a bell upside down), and from this bell all round the cap projects foliage, and this type is known by that name. This form is well shown in the carved cap from Aldingbourne (Fig. 57), in which, moreover, the abacus is no longer square along its edge, but moulded, as shown more

FIG. 58. SECTION
OF CAP, ALDINGBOURNE

FIG. 57. A WELL-CARVED TRANSITIONAL CAP
FROM ALDINGBOURNE. 1185

clearly in the section through the upper part of the cap in Fig. 58, for it would be out of keeping to have a heavy square stone forming the upper part of a cap whilst the remainder was so delicately carved.

Lightness takes the place of heaviness, the cap is just as strong as the Norman cushion cap, but it is altogether more graceful and beautiful.

The detail sketch from Yapton (Fig. 59) shows more clearly how tentative at first were the efforts to develop the carving in the first stage, showing part of an ornament, only one-half of which was ever finished, and it may be seen thus to this day ; it is quite an interesting example, showing that all these developments were never anything else than gradual. The more developed specimen (Fig. 60) is an early form of what is known as a Boss, and, as here shown, occurs at the corner of the cap (Fig. 60), and is decidedly Early English in character.

Compare the two sections of bases given from Yapton (Fig. 61) and Pagham (Fig. 62) and you will note the shallowness of the one and the more developed shape and depth of the other. The former is only a little removed from the Norman in design, whilst the latter is approaching full Early English.

The square end of the wall at Pagham (Fig. 63) may be described as a pier. It is not left absolutely square, as it would have been by the Normans. The corners are cut away, and small columns are formed at the angles. It has been transformed, beautified, and lightened. The bases are more interesting with their deeper mouldings. The caps are deeply carved with a stiff-leaved foliage. In this particular instance the arch projects over the pier below in a curious way, as if the Normans had built the arch so that it rested on a thick, solid pier, and then the later builders had come along and cut back the pier and moulded and ornamented it. The abacus is partly square above and moulded below, and the " bell " of the cap is profusely ornamented with carving.

This actual instance of transition in the making is extremely interesting. What it actually represents is this : The Normans built a thick, rather uninterest-

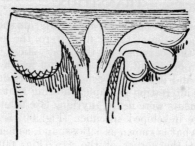

FIG. 59. AN EARLY FORM OF CARVING, FROM A CAP AT YAPTON, SUSSEX.
ITS UNFINISHED STATE SHOWS US SOMETHING OF THE MIND OF THE CARVER.
1160–1200

FIG. 61. A TRANSITIONAL
BASE FROM YAPTON, SUSSEX.
1160–1200

FIG. 60. A FURTHER DEVELOP-
MENT OF CARVING FROM A CAP AT
YAPTON. 1160–1200

FIG. 62. SECTION OF THE BASE,
PAGHAM

ing wall or pier, and left it probably with a plain cap and base. It remained thus for a number of years. Then, later on in the Transition period, the stone-

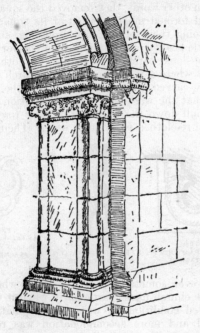

FIG. 63. A TRANSITION TREATMENT OF A PIER, SHOWING A TENDENCY TO LIGHTEN WHAT WOULD OTHERWISE BE A HEAVY AND SOLID MASS OF STONE-WORK. THERE ARE SMALL COLUMNS AT THE CORNERS. THE ABACUS IS MOULDED, THE BELL OF THE CAP IS CARVED, AND THE BASE IS WELL MOULDED. PAGHAM, SUSSEX. 1185

masons of the day thought they would relieve this solid mass in some way. They had no need to pull it down and thus interfere with the use of the church,

and they could not do much to the arch, for fear of
weakening the building. They simply carved away
portions of it—those portions that they could easily
reach ; in other words, they removed the square edges
of it and formed mouldings out of its square edges.
By so doing they formed caps, columns, and bases
of no little beauty out of the existing masonry.

If you look carefully you will see other such
instances where a thick, heavy-looking arch rests on
delicately carved columns. It will then be obvious
to you that the workmen in one generation did not
always pull down the buildings of their forefathers,
but often re-clothed them, as it were. Their succes-

FIG. 64.
PLAN OF HALF THE
BASE AT PAGHAM

FIG. 65.
SECTION OF CAPITAL
AT PAGHAM

FIG. 66
AN ENLARGED SKETCH
OF A CARVED BOSS
FRAGMENT FROM
PAGHAM

sors, however, sometimes pulled down the whole wall,
if not the church itself, particularly when it was in a
dilapidated condition, or when the population had
increased and more accommodation was required.
They then rebuilt after their own manner—a manner
based partly on the constructive experience and
partly on the methods of execution employed by their
immediate predecessors of the end of the Norman period,
evolving from both an even more developed style.
And so the progress goes *gradually* on.

The plan of the base at Pagham (Fig. 64) shows
how the square corner of the pier has been cut away

and a little column formed, and also how the base mouldings have been worked round to correspond.

The section through the abacus (Fig. 65) from the same church gives a good idea of the early simple development of the upper part of the cap.

The carved fragment (Fig. 66) shows a very conventional treatment, something between a flower and a foliage type. This was a very favourite form, and we shall see something very much like it in the succeeding Early English style.

The North Mundham example of a cap (Fig. 67) is very advanced, but you will note that the whole cap (abacus and bell) is moulded, and there is here

FIG. 67. SECTION AND PART FRONT VIEW OF A WELL-DEVELOPED CAP FROM NORTH MUNDHAM, SUSSEX, DATED 1210, WHICH MAY BE DESCRIBED AS EITHER TRANSITION OR FULLY DEVELOPED EARLY ENGLISH. THE ABACUS (UPPER PART) AND THE BELL (LOWER PART) OF THE CAP ARE BOTH DEEPLY UNDERCUT

no ornamental carving of any description. This moulded cap was kept up in all the different periods independent of the ornamental types.

In the larger sketch of a pier at Aldingbourne (Fig. 68) you will note some interesting features of the Transition. Looking first at the left-hand side of the sketch, you will find an Early English form of pointed arch. This rests on a rather solid three-

E

quarter column (Fig. 69), reminiscent of the Norman method in its solidity, the cap being a glorified version of the Norman scalloped cap, with a kind of fluting carried round it. Attached to the side of the larger column is a smaller and more slender half

FIG. 68. ALDINGBOURNE, SUSSEX. DATE, 1190. SHOWING A TRANSITIONAL GROWTH FROM THE HEAVY ROUND NORMAN COLUMN TO THE LIGHTER CARVED HALF COLUMN AT THE SIDE, AND ALSO A FURTHER STAGE OF PROGRESS IN THE POINTED VAULTED STONE CEILING ENRICHED BY THE DOG-TOOTHED ORNAMENT

column, which is obviously there in order to help to support the stone ceiling.

The distant part of the view shows vaulting, in which the groins, where the vaulting surfaces intersect, are emphasized by projecting stones or ribs. The Normans would have left the ribs plain, but these more advanced thinkers introduced mouldings, then, as we have seen, carved a dog-tooth ornament amongst them with rather a happy result, as shown in the more detailed sketch (Fig. 70). Smaller ribs were also carried round the edge of the vaulting where it meets the wall.

FIG. 69. PLAN OF LARGE ROUND COLUMN, WITH SMALLER HALF ROUND COLUMN AT THE SIDE. ALDINGBOURNE

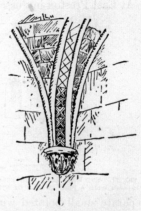

FIG. 70. ALDINGBOURNE, SUSSEX. SPRINGING OF VAULT, 1190

WINDOWS.—Although mouldings and ornament are perhaps some of the best guides as to the style and date of a building, the windows, and particularly the shape of them, are equally distinctive.

We noted in the Saxon style that occasionally two windows were brought close together and only divided by a small column or baluster. The Normans, however, did not necessarily begin where the Saxons left off, but arrived at the same result later in their period. In other words, they began with the use of single windows, and either put solid arches on either side (Fig. 28) or grouped these windows closer together, as we see below. Thus history repeats itself, but it does so unconsciously after an interval.

Let us look at Transition windows and those that follow. Figs. 71, 72, and 73 show three methods of introducing light by means of windows, into a building.

At East Preston in Sussex (Fig. 71), there are three

FIG. 71. END WALL FROM EAST PRESTON, SUSSEX. A GROUPING OF THREE WINDOWS WITH A FAIR AMOUNT OF STONEWORK IN BETWEEN EACH WINDOW

separate small pointed windows with a fair amount of walling in between each window.

In the second example, from Clymping (Fig. 72), you will note that in addition to the three windows being close together there are two little windows, or "lights," as I ought more properly to call them, inserted above. This is rather an important development to which I shall have good reason to refer later at more length, but we begin already to see interesting possibilities.

In the third sketch, from Bosham (Fig. 73), as many as five " lights " are brought together, quite closely, under the one arch, and the stone divisions between are treated as delicate columns. This example is full Early English.

I will now give some notes of the historical changes of which this transition in architecture was but a reflection.

In this Transition period, I have been dealing with the work which was carried out in the reign of Henry II, Richard I, and John.

There were rebellions and invasions during these times, but it must be remembered that now, under Henry II particularly, were laid the foundations of our Common Law, and so conditions were more

FIG. 72. AN INTERIOR VIEW OF WINDOWS FROM CLYMPING, SUSSEX, HAVING ABOVE THEM TWO SUNK PANELS, WHICH LATER IN THE STYLE WOULD BE PIERCED AS LIGHTS AND GRADUALLY, LATER STILL, THE STONEWORK BETWEEN THE SMALL LIGHTS AND THE LARGER ONES WOULD BECOME LESS AND LESS, FORMING A DESIGN, KNOWN AS TRACERY, IN THE STONEWORK

FIG. 73. THE FIVE WINDOWS AT BOSHAM (INTERIOR VIEW) ARE GROUPED VERY CLOSELY, LEAVING A MERE STRIP OF STONEWORK IN BETWEEN. THE STRIPS BECOME COLUMNS

orderly and building work could go ahead more easily. Richard I took part in the Third Crusade. And we are thus reminded that Christianity was not the only religious creed, for these Crusades by the Christians were directed against the Mohammedan Turks of Palestine.

In this Eastern warfare our English kings would doubtless notice many new ideas and forms of construction, and would introduce them here on their return. The Temple Church, London, and the

Church of the Holy Sepulchre, Cambridge, both with naves round in plan, show that in some cases the actual plan of the church was affected by this Eastern influence ; but the newer ideas as to construction and detail were also incorporated throughout the land.

We come next to a break—though only a short one—in the continuity of English church building. In the reign of King John, Stephen Langton was appointed Archbishop of Canterbury by the Pope of Rome. The King objected and a quarrel ensued between King and Pope. As a result the latter, in 1208, laid England under an interdict and John was excommunicated. During this interdict most of the churches were closed, and for a few years nothing could be done in the way of building parish churches. Thus no further development took place in the evolution of style. Then, later, John surrendered the country to the Pope, and after perpetual quarrels with his barons eventually put his seal to the Magna Charta, and both church and social matters were, therefore, somewhat straightened, better conditions prevailed, and the repair and building of churches once again progressed, as we shall see in the next chapter.

SUMMARY

TRANSITION

1. WALLS.—Masses of stonework, relieved by mouldings and often carving. Ends of walls frequently had small columns attached.
2. BUTTRESSES.—Made more slender in proportions. Sometimes moulded.
3. COLUMNS.—Thinner caps with moulded abacus

and carved bell, moulded bases. Columns often
detached, i.e. not necessarily joined to the wall.

4. DOORWAYS.—Some with round arches, some
with pointed. Moulded, occasionally with dog-
tooth. Several arches, within one another,
with columns under the jambs.

5. WINDOWS.—Some pointed, some round-headed.
Two or three sometimes brought together with
but little stonework in between.

6. MOULDINGS.—Lighter and more elegant. More
deeply cut.

7. ORNAMENT.—Dog-tooth in an early form, carved
foliage to the caps. Foliage of "stiff-leaf"
type.

8. VAULTING.—Often pointed. Ribs at the inter-
section were occasionally moulded and ornamented. These were supported by slender
columns, often of marble.

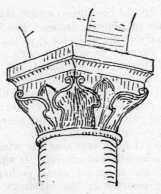

FIG. 73A. WATER-LEAF CAPITAL, A TRANSITION TYPE

CHAPTER V

GOTHIC I

EARLY ENGLISH (ABOUT 1200–1250)

THE preceding Transition style and the one we are now about to consider together cover the hundred years whose central point is the year 1200, and this EARLY ENGLISH period carries our history down well into the middle of Henry III's reign.

The title given to this period is well chosen, for with the confirmation of the Great Charter the history of the English nation may well be said to have commenced, and the fusion of the English with their Norman conquerors completed.

This is the first of the three GOTHIC styles, and is essentially one of pointed arches. We have done with the Norman round arch, for it is displaced by a development wherein, we may say with much truth, the apex of Mediaeval Art is reached.

The general effect is now, in both mass and detail, a combination of scientific construction with lightness and elegance, possessing a tendency always to carry the eye upward, with a beauty which remains unsurpassed in any subsequent age.

BUTTRESSES.—I have said that the windows have a great deal to do with our subject. It will be easily understood that, as more (and perhaps larger) windows were inserted in the buildings, the walls would have a tendency to become weakened. This was counteracted by giving more prominence to the buttress, which, as we have already learnt, strengthens the wall. These buttresses also helped to take the additional weight from the roofs and vaults. We find that the ribs of the vaulting were so arranged that its weight was concentrated in certain places, just as any arch form, particularly a pointed one, would throw the weight to that point in the wall where the arch commenced or " sprang." I shall refer again to this important question of vaulting later on, but at the moment it suffices to say that the slightly projecting and somewhat crude buttress of the Normans became much more important and had a greater projection in this period, particularly at its base near the ground, as at Higham Ferrers (Fig. 74).

FIG. 74.
EARLY ENGLISH
BUTTRESS,
HIGHAM FERRERS

WALLS.—Owing to this greater ingenuity in resting the roofs on the points where buttresses occur, and to greater care exercised in building the walls, these were now thinner than in the Norman time ; for a well-built thin wall, if buttressed at points where the pressures are collected, is stronger than a thicker wall built of loosely assembled stones bearing a continuous weight.

WINDOWS.—In this style we have not only the grouping of windows already referred to (Fig. 73), but also the germ of what later developed into wonderful types of "fenestration," or window arrangement, for more and more of the wall space was given up to windows. First of all, I must mention the narrow single windows, often found in

small country churches. They are given the name
Lancet, owing to their high, narrow, and pointed
form (Fig. 75). Notice the development. Besides
being placed singly, these windows were placed in
pairs or threes, or even in fives, as we saw at Bosham
(Fig. 73). But the point is, that when they were
thus brought together they were often placed under
the one main arch.

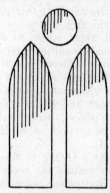

FIG. 75. LANCET

FIG. 76. TWO LANCETS WITH
ONE CIRCULAR LIGHT OVER

TRACERY.—I will explain the gradual evolution
which followed, leading up to what is known as
WINDOW TRACERY, which was indeed an important
development. This term TRACERY is used to denote
the form which the stonework took between the
various parts of a window. Fig. 76 does not show
tracery, because there are three separate windows;
but Fig. 77 does, because there are three parts to the
one window, and the intervening stonework is only
slight.

PLATE TRACERY.—As the style developed, then,

two windows were brought together as a "two-light" window; at first one round light was arranged above it (Fig. 76), then later all three lights were united as one window under one main arch (Fig. 77), but still leaving a flat " plate " of stone between the lights. This development is therefore known as PLATE TRACERY, and was fully developed in this

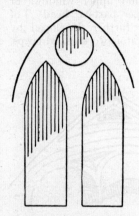

FIG. 77. THREE LIGHTS UNDER
ONE ARCH. PLATE TRACERY

FIG. 78. LESS STONEWORK
BETWEEN THE LIGHTS. BAR
TRACERY

style. It soon died out, however, and is rarely found in any other period.

BAR TRACERY.—Later on the stonework between the parts became considerably narrower, and by its thinness gave the appearance of bars of stonework. This tracery is known then as BAR TRACERY (Fig. 78), which takes us to the beginning of the Decorated style and was the only kind developed in subsequent styles.

It is at times not easy to distinguish the bar

tracery of this period from that of the next, but there is no difficulty if you will bear in mind that, although the work of this style was of superb beauty, it was essentially simple. The bars in the bar tracery of the succeeding period were often twisted and turned for the sake of effect; this never occurred in the Early English style.

CUSPING.—These little round upper windows or lights, together with the upper parts ("heads") of the lights below, were later further developed by means of projecting points of stonework called cusps,

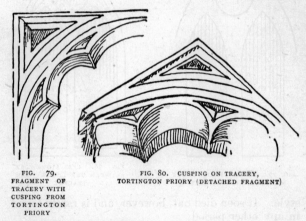

FIG. 79.
FRAGMENT OF
TRACERY WITH
CUSPING FROM
TORTINGTON
PRIORY

FIG. 80.   CUSPING ON TRACERY,
TORTINGTON PRIORY (DETACHED FRAGMENT)

as shown in the fragment from Tortington Priory (Figs. 79, 80), of later date, but clearly indicating the point under discussion.

The curved spaces formed *between* the points or Cusps are called foils or leaves, and it is usual to designate the design by the number of leaves formed. Cusped openings are therefore described as either being trefoil (three-leaved), quatrefoil (four-leaved), cinquefoil (five-leaved), or multifoil (many-leaved). For example, the sketch from Chester (Fig. 81) shows in its upper part a quatrefoil, that is, four leaves formed by four cusps ; in the lower part a trefoil is formed by two cusps, the half divisions at each side being counted each as one.

The presence of cusping denotes that the work was

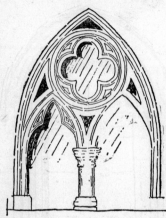

FIG. 81. FROM CHESTER CATHEDRAL. *c.* 1250. TWO POINTED LIGHTS WITH ONE CIRCULAR OPENING ABOVE, AND TREATED SO AS TO FORM FULLY DEVELOPED BAR TRACERY

well on in this period ; the cusps sometimes formed part of the stone framework of the window and at other times were separate stones let into the inner edges of the bars.

In connexion with the development of windows in this style it must be here mentioned that the art of painted glass—an interesting subject dealt with in Chapter XIII—was now being more fully developed. The glass worker would see that the mason gave as much accommodation as possible for the display of this craft, which later developed into the crowning glory of our church architecture.

DOORWAYS.—The doorways of this period are nearly always pointed, though sometimes of trefoil form, with rounded top, and the arch was usually well moulded. In the example from Merstham in Surrey (Fig. 82) you will note that the main arch is

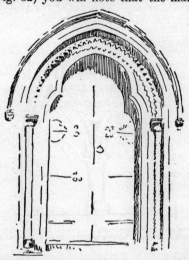

FIG. 82. MERSTHAM, SURREY. 1190–1210. EARLY ENGLISH DOORWAY WITH SMALL COLUMNS IN ANGLES. POINTED ARCH WITH DOG-TOOTH ORNAMENT

made up of a number of mouldings. The outer one, right on the face of the wall, is known as a label or Hood mould, a simpler form of which we saw in an earlier period (Fig. 29). This moulding would have a tendency to carry away the rain, running down the wall from above, clear of the actual door. The next moulding, formed in the wall, is merely rounded off, a type of moulding I shall refer to later. The next moulding is enriched by the Early English dog-tooth, which springs from a little column on each side, slightly worn by time; their caps and bases were once delicately moulded in stones built into the wall behind, but the shaft is an independent stone clear of the wall. Finally there is another rounded moulding in trefoil form, i.e. bent out to form two cusps.

COLUMNS.—As the style develops the detached columns become more common; they also become longer, but the thickness remains the same; and we shall note that the long slender column is sometimes strengthened by an intermediate moulded band, half way up its height, between the moulded cap and the moulded base. This band is built into the wall in the same way as are the cap and the base, for strength.

ARCADES.—The arches and columns supporting them, forming the main arcades between the nave and the aisles, carry out the idea of the pointed arch, and the greater profusion of columns and mouldings. The arrangement of the columns with their moulded arches is like the doorway treatment already referred to, but

FIG. 83

on a larger and more profuse scale. There is often a fair-sized central column with a cluster of smaller columns around the main column (Fig. 83), each smaller column having its own set of mouldings in the arch over, as it did in the doorways.

But it must be borne in mind that in many small churches which are treated in a simple manner, in whatever style they are built, one round or even octagonal column would suffice, and that when we are trying to date a building, or trying to place it in regard to the various styles, we shall not be quite sure in which period it was built until we have

examined the detail of the caps and bases. Thus in
a small church with a small arch of few mouldings
a single central column would suffice. It would still

FIG. 84. LINCOLN. 1280. STIFF-LEAF FOLIAGE

be Early English if the shape of the mouldings of the
arch, cap, or base were characteristic of that period.

If, however, the set of arch mouldings is sufficiently
elaborate to be divided up into groups of mouldings

we shall find that there will be a little column under each group, and the example may then be considered as fully developed.

Thus one may find in the arcade of a fairly large church a central column surrounded by perhaps four slender columns or shafts (Fig. 83), but there would be a combined cap for the group and a combined base for the group.

CAPS AND BASES.—The caps and bases are always well moulded, and in addition many of the caps are ornamented with carving, as at Lincoln, which happens to be a well-advanced example (Fig. 84).

Generally, as here, the upper part of the cap or abacus (now generally circular, not square on plan, i.e. looking down from above), consists of overhanging rounds and deep hollows, perhaps divided by very small square portions. The bell portion or lower part of the cap is sometimes plain, but is often characteristically carved with representations of stiff-leaved foliage, as we saw in the last period.

MOULDINGS.—I have referred to mouldings as I have dealt with the various features on which they occur, but it is important to note here what their actual characteristics are. If you refer to Fig. 90 you will see that the upper edge of the abacus is not square as usual in previous styles, but rounded off ; there is, however, a square portion known as a fillet on the front ; then in the upper part of Fig. 84, on the right hand side, you will see that the round is brought to a sharp point, this is known as a pointed Bowtell or Keel moulding.

There are therefore three varieties of round or roll mouldings :

> (a) Plain roll.
> (b) Filleted roll.
> (c) Pointed roll.

These rounds or rolls alternate with deep hollows. Fillets or square portions are freely interspersed.

STIFF-LEAF FOLIAGE.—This is, as we have seen, a kind of foliage, in stone, branching from stiff stalks.

In its early form this particular carving might well lead one to imagine an attempt at representing, in stone, a clenched hand with thumb and knuckles curved outwards from a wrist.

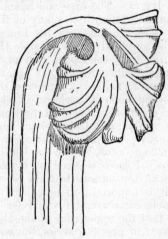

FIG. 85.   EARLY ENGLISH CARVING.   BOSS FROM A CAP IN YORK MINSTER.
ABOUT 1240–1260

The larger sketch from York Minster (Fig. 85) is a fairly early form and should be referred to as a Boss.

The sectional sketch shows the relative position of boss to the bell of the capital (Fig. 90).

The stiff-leaved carving from Hexham (Fig. 86) shows again how simple the form may be at times. This is nevertheless quite a characteristic piece of carving.

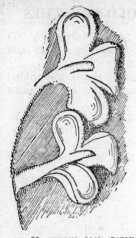

FIG. 86. HEXHAM. 1240. EARLY ENGLISH STIFF-LEAF CARVING. PROJECTING LESS THAN ONE INCH FROM A FLAT WALL SURFACE

FIG. 87. SEDILIA BRACKET. ALDINGBOURNE

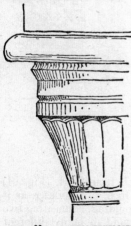

FIG. 88. A WELL-DEVELOPED MOULDED CORBEL OR PROJECTION, FROM YAPTON, DATED 1210, WHICH IS PRACTICALLY EARLY ENGLISH IN STYLE AND DATE

FIG. 89. SECTION. TYPICAL EARLY ENGLISH BASE. YORK. 1240-1260

The bracket or corbel from Aldingbourne (Fig. 87) shows a series of mouldings, including rounds and hollows—with the dog-tooth in the latter.

The cap from Yapton (Fig. 88) shows a moulded abacus with a developed form of the old Norman scallop.

The base of the Early English column—that is, its lower end, near the floor—is always formed like, or is a variation of, the one at York (Fig. 89). The hollow portion is cut deep down and could "hold water."

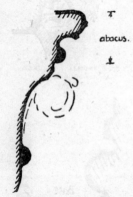

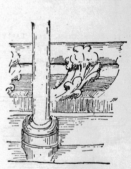

FIG. 91.   CROCKET AT SIDE OF COLUMN.   YORK, 1216–1255

FIG. 90.   SECTION THROUGH A WELL-MOULDED EARLY ENGLISH CAP WITH MOULDED ABACUS.   THE BELL OR REMAINING PART OF THE CAP IS FILLED WITH CARVED STIFF LEAF FOLIAGE, WITH BOLDLY PROJECTING BOSSES.   YORK, 1240–1260

CROCKET.—The other sketch from York (Fig. 91) shows, behind the column, a form of CROCKET, as it was carved across a hollow moulding, connecting two round mouldings, but it is found in many different positions.

Dog-Tooth.—I now come to the fully-developed dog-tooth ornament, which has already asserted itself, in a primitive form, well before its proper time.

The sectional view (Fig. 92) shows columns grouped, in the way we now expect to find them, in the jamb of a large door at Lichfield, supporting several sets of arch mouldings.

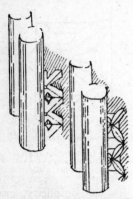

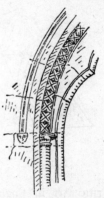

FIG. 92. DOORWAY AT LICHFIELD, SHOWING CLUSTERED COLUMNS OR SHAFTS, BEHIND ONE OF WHICH AND AT THE SIDE OF ANOTHER WILL BE FOUND CONTINUOUS VERTICAL LINES OF DOG-TOOTH ORNAMENT

FIG. 93. SIDE OF EARLY ENGLISH DOOR, SHOWING DOG-TOOTH ORNAMENT

At the moment we are not concerned with the arch, but as to what we find at the side of the door and behind these columns. Here we have two or three vertical rows of this characteristic dog-tooth behind and between the columns, and I give several views (Figs. 93–95) so as to make its form clearer. The form treatment slightly varies not only in various parts of the country, but sometimes in the same building built at the one time.

In one of the rows (Fig. 95) the ornament is placed obliquely and out of centre in order to bring its point behind the centre of the column (Fig. 92).

These are the little variations and surprises which add interest and no little charm to our subject.

The end of this period and the beginning of the succeeding one, the DECORATED, mark the summit of

FIG. 94. LOOK-
ING DOWN ON
EARLY ENGLISH
DOG-TOOTH ORNA-
MENT.

FIG. 95. DOG-TOOTH,
PURPOSELY CARVED UN-
SYMMETRICALLY, S O
THAT THE POINT OF THE
ORNAMENT COMES BE-
HIND A COLUMN. (See
Fig. 92)

GOTHIC Art in England, for the simplicity, grace, beauty, and sense of truthfulness met with in old churches of this time achieve a greatness unequalled in any other period and unsurpassed in any other country.

The arches, columns, and details have developed into something full of character and beauty, but not only this, the arrangement of the church itself is now of special interest. This general aspect of the whole building is dealt with in Chapter VIII.

SUMMARY

EARLY ENGLISH

1. GENERALLY.—The first of the Gothic styles. A lighter and more scientific construction, producing a more beautiful effect.
2. WALLS.—Thinner, but better built than previously.
3. BUTTRESSES.—Important. Greater projection.
4. OPENINGS.—Always pointed arches.
5. WINDOWS.—Lancet. Plain or moulded, together with small columns at sides. Tracery: first, plate tracery then bar tracery, both the outcome of close grouping of "lights." Cusping fully developed.
6. DOORWAYS.—Well moulded. A series of arches, with small columns in the jambs. Hood mould.
7. COLUMNS.—Slender; if very slender, strengthened by bands. In arcades, one thick central column is often surrounded by four slender shafts. Octagonal columns survive in small churches.
8. CAPS AND BASES.—Deeply moulded, often ornamented with stiff-leaf ornaments. Bases are deeply incut so as to "hold water."
9. MOULDINGS.—Rounds and hollows (deep); the former may be either plain roll, filleted roll, or pointed roll.
10. ORNAMENT.—Stiff-leaf foliage. Dog-tooth. Crockets.

CHAPTER VI

GOTHIC II

DECORATED

Including Geometrical 1250–1320, *Flowing* 1320–1360

THE hundred years covering this style approxi-
mates roughly to the reigns of the three first
Edwards.

During this time there were wars with Scotland and
Wales. The Hundred Years War with France was
commenced. But between these troubled intervals
the people, particularly the middle classes, were living
under improved conditions, mainly brought about by
the first popularly represented Parliament.

Edward I concentrated on England rather than
foreign countries ; there was more or less peace at
home and certainly commercial prosperity. The
Church, too, was prosperous. Although the period
commenced well, however, its prosperity did not last,
for Edward II did not inherit his father's wisdom,
and so we find the conditions of the life of the people
reflected in their architecture. The simplicity and
the beauty of Early English architecture gave way to
the more elaborate Decorated, and this in turn
declined at the time when the Church and the people
were over-prosperous. Last of all, we come to the
second definite break—this time a serious one, in the
continuity of building—the terrible Black Death,

which devastated the country in 1349. This stopped, at the zenith of its extravagant variety, all building, civil as well as ecclesiastical. It is only in East Anglia that this style persists much beyond the year 1350.

WINDOWS.—I will first deal with windows, for in buildings of this period we shall first of all notice a striking difference in their size.

They were not only much larger, but they were broader than in the preceding style. We have left the narrow lancet form and now find that the churches were given much more glass area, not only because most of the fighting was done elsewhere and the necessity of defending the buildings of a town or village was therefore gone, but because it was now becoming more fashionable to fill the church windows with stained glass; this would shut out a certain amount of light, but the loss would be made up by having a greater window area. Bar tracery was now ready to be developed to the best advantage. The varieties of forms into which it could be twisted were legion; it became a framework for stained glass, but, owing to the size of the window, had now to withstand no small amount of wind pressure during gales.

In the Early English period we saw early uses of bar tracery (see Fig. 81). In the example from Dorchester, Oxon (Fig. 96) we have a more developed form of window, which explains the sub-title of our style, GEOMETRICAL. In this type of tracery the bars of stonework dividing the various lights were turned and shaped to give a geometrical pattern, in many cases of much beauty.

The upright dividing bars are called MULLIONS.

In the later example from Ford Church, Sussex (Fig. 97) the same idea occurs, though in this case the pattern formed is distinctly FLOWING and not

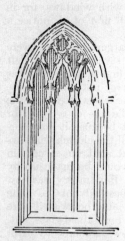

FIG. 96. FROM DORCHESTER,
OXON. DATED 1300. BAR
TRACERY IN A FORM KNOWN
AS GEOMETRICAL, FOUND IN
THE EARLIER PART OF THE
DECORATED PERIOD. THE
CUSPING, OR OUTWARD-POINT-
ING PORTIONS OF STONE-WORK,
IS PART OF THE TRACERY IN
THIS STYLE

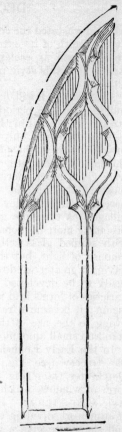

FIG. 97. A FLOWING FORM OF
TRACERY, FROM FORD CHURCH,
SUSSEX, MET WITH IN THE LATER
PART OF THE DECORATED STYLE.
SOME OF THE FLOWING FORMS
HAVE A BEAUTIFUL EFFECT, BUT
IN MANY CASES THE RESULT IS
MEANINGLESS AS THE TRACERY IS
TWISTED AND TURNED FOR ITS
OWN SAKE

geometrical. This flowing form generally denotes the Later Decorated, and some of the examples to be found are somewhat striking and usually very fine.

But the windows in this flowing period become very elaborate, an elaboration which makes itself felt throughout the church in the detail and ornament, which often one cannot help feeling is overdone ; its effusiveness, and sometimes fussiness, leaves the mind confused, for there is not the meaning in it now that there was in the earlier and simpler designs. For instance, in the Early English period we found that the design of the window was evolved naturally by bringing two or three windows together and making the stonework between less and less ; but now, in this style this narrow stonework was twisted into patterns for their own sake, and their original constructional meaning was lost.

This ornamentation used for the sake of ornamentation is a sign of deterioration.

BUTTRESSES.—Whereas in churches of the Early English period the corner of the building would be treated with two buttresses running out at right

FIG. 98

angles (Fig. 98) in the Decorated style they would be set obliquely (Fig. 98), a method which is not quite so strong, but strong enough. The whole essence of Gothic construction is that every stone is the right size, of the most suitable shape, and placed in the most useful position.

The ordinary buttresses, not at the corners, were still more important ; for the walls, further weakened by wider windows, would require extra strengthening by deeper buttresses.

Now, in spite of the fact that many of the churches built in this Decorated period answer well to this descriptive title, we must not be surprised to find not a few examples up and down the country which, though built at this time, are very simple and plain, for this elaboration would be costly and could not always be afforded. There is many a little church, perhaps in a secluded spot such as at Dunsfold in Surrey, with its broader windows and its distinctive mouldings and ornament, with but very little else to show that it belongs to this period.

These are often very delightful churches to visit.

Whether the example be plain or profuse, the work of this time is generally very fascinating and attractive, but the novice is inclined when considering the more elaborate churches to be carried away with what is actually not so very far removed from a jazz result, produced by an overpowering surfeit of carving ; for the function of carving should be to relieve an otherwise bareness of wall, and not to overpower by its prominence the general structure of the building.

COLUMNS.—The clustered columns of the main nave arcades are now infrequent, but an interesting effect is obtained by attaching four half columns to a main central square pier or column (Fig. 103). We shall also find a single column octagonal on plan as in the Early English style.

DOORWAYS.—In the example given of the doorway to the porch at Amberley (Fig. 99) in Sussex you will note that the sides or jambs are moulded as before, with little columns, but *the columns themselves are moulded*, and it is not easy to see where mouldings and columns start and finish (Figs. 99 and 102).

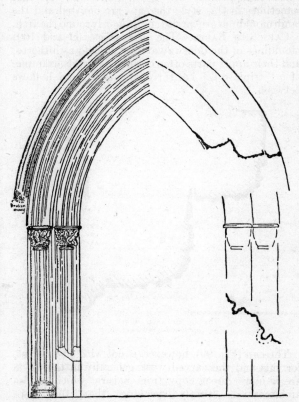

FIG. 99. A DECORATED PERIOD DOORWAY FROM AMBERLEY, SUSSEX, SHOWING SHALLOW BUT NUMEROUS MOULDINGS, EVEN THE SMALL COLUMNS BEING SO MOULDED AS TO LOSE SOMETHING OF THEIR FUNCTION. THE CAPS ARE CARVED TO REPRESENT NATURAL FOLIAGE

The original ideas are thus again lost. In fact sometimes in this style the caps are omitted and the jamb mouldings are carried continuously round the arch.

CAPS AND BASES.—The base (Figs. 99 and 100) mouldings of the doorway are not so bold as hitherto, and their upper parts often consist, as in this example, of a " triple roll," i.e. three rounds without hollows between.

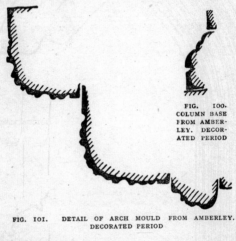

FIG. 100. COLUMN BASE FROM AMBER-LEY. DECOR-ATED PERIOD

FIG. 101. DETAIL OF ARCH MOULD FROM AMBERLEY. DECORATED PERIOD

The cap (Fig. 99), however, is not without interest, for this and the carved work generally in this style are a more direct copy from nature, which is less architectural, strictly speaking, than the more formal stiff-leaf ; for really a design should, to be successful, be conventionalized to suit the material in which it is executed. The abacus of the cap is often octagonal on plan. Caps are sometimes omitted altogether.

Mouldings.—Note particularly the mouldings to the arch over the doorway (Figs. 99 and 101); they are very poor and shallow. Each set (for there are two sets) is made up of shallow mouldings and not deep ones. The outer moulding of all is the Hood mould. Further mouldings are given at the end of the Summary.

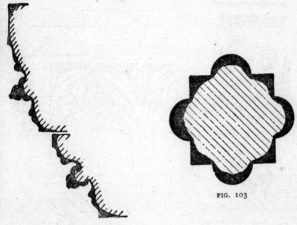

FIG. 103

FIG. 102.   DETAIL OF JAMB OR SIDE OF DOORWAY, SHOWING MOULDED COLUMNS, AMBERLEY. DECORATED PERIOD

Ornament.—*Ball-Flower*: In addition to the natural foliage there is used in this style an ornament known as the BALL-FLOWER (Fig. 104). This will be found, as the dog-tooth was found in the earlier style, in between mouldings or on mouldings; it is, however, extremely decorative but at times is overdone, and in some cases its repetition is decidedly monotonous. It may be found covering the bars of the tracery of a large window. It is a round ball or sphere with a portion of its upper surface carved away as if it were intended to represent a round bud about to burst open.

CROCKET.—In this period also great use was made, decoratively, of the crocket, as at Dorchester (Fig. 105) ; but the design of this was more elaborate than in the preceding style and may be described as

FIG. 104. THE BALL-FLOWER ORNAMENT, VERY PREVALENT IN THE DECORATED PERIOD

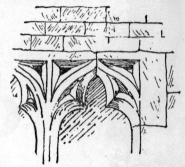

FIG. 106. SQUARE-HEADED OPENING AMBERLEY CASTLE, *c.* 1330

FIG. 105. DECORATED CROCKET. DORCHESTER, OXON

a flowing crocket. It was often placed at intervals on the sloping edge of a roof gable, or round the hood-mould of an opening.

SQUARE-HEADED OPENING.—We now meet practically for the first time with the square-headed opening as shown at Amberley Castle (Fig. 106). It must be mentioned here, although it was more common in the succeeding Perpendicular style. Its form is no exact criterion as to whether it belongs to this or the next style, and the tracery under it is the only guide.

OGEE ARCH.—Occasionally an ogee head is found, and is specially characteristic of this period. This consists in bringing up the head of the arch to a sharp point by means of curving it in a double way as at Ford, Sussex (Fig. 107). The lines of this form of arch are certainly graceful, but it is asking rather much of the arch to twist it in this way. You thereby lose the principle of an arch, for if an arch has the direction of its main curve suddenly reversed it will be weakened in that part where the reversing takes place. In other words, a normal arch is strong

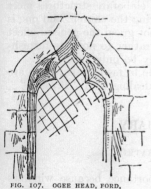

FIG. 107. OGEE HEAD, FORD, SUSSEX. DECORATED PERIOD

FIG. 108. CANOPIED TOMB BOSHAM.

because the pressure of one wedge-shaped stone on another is continuous in its direction; this is the true function of a proper arch, and if the direction of the curve is suddenly reversed, as in the ogee form, its strength has gone and the result is successful neither practically nor visually. In a small arch, as shown, both curves are worked on the one piece of stone and no great harm is done; but imagine the resulting weakness in a larger arch than the one I show.

G

MEMORIALS AND TOMBS.—These become more important in this period, and the opportunity to make these decorative was certainly not lost. Many are very beautiful. A tomb may have its own little stone roof, or, if it is placed in a recess, the wall above may be treated as a roof or canopy. These canopies were often treated as miniature churches in their design, with small but elaborate groined roofs, moulded sides and bases, all profusely ornamented. An example is given from Bosham (Fig. 108). They should not, however, distract one's attention from the church itself, for these elaborate structures meet the eye at once upon entering the church, and one is inclined to see these and not grasp the general effect of the main building, but rather to note its furnishings, which should properly be only subsidiary.

Further reference is made to memorials, which are important, in the chapter dealing with "Brasses."

SUMMARY

DECORATED

1. WALLS.—Of less importance because windows were larger.
2. BUTTRESS.—Important for the same reason. Corner buttresses set diagonally. Treated with ornament characteristic of the period.
3. OPENINGS.—Wider; covered by wider-pointed arches. Occasionally ogee arched, square-headed.
4. WINDOWS.—Formed of a FLOWING and GEOMETRICAL tracery.
5. DOORWAYS.—Wider. Many small shallow mouldings in the arch. Jambs treated with

mouldings and *moulded* columns. Sometimes there is no intervening cap between arch and jamb mouldings.

6. COLUMNS.—In arcades, centre square column with four half-columns attached to it is common. Octagonal columns for small churches.

7. CAPS.—Moulded abacus, often octagonal on plan, natural carving to the bell or lower part of cap.

8. BASES.—Shallow quarter-roll mouldings without hollows, such as " triple roll."

9. MOULDINGS.—Succession of shallow quarter rounds, few hollows. Some square fillets. Varieties found : scroll or roll with projecting

FIG. 109.
SCROLL OR
ROLL, WITH
PROJECTING
EDGE LIKE
A SCROLL OF
PAPER

FIG. 110.
OGEE, A
MOULDING
CURVED FIRST
INWARD AND
THEN OUT-
WARD

FIG. 111.
BRACKET OR
BRACE MOULD-
ING

edge like a scroll of paper (Fig. 109); bracket or brace moulding (Fig. 111); also ogee (Fig. 110).

10. ORNAMENT.—Ball-flower. Flowing crocket. Natural foliage, e.g. oak, ivy, vine, etc.

CHAPTER VII

GOTHIC III

PERPENDICULAR (1360–1485)

WE have now come to the last of the three
Gothic styles, and the one that is confined to
these islands. The previous styles had their counter-
part to a more or less degree on the Continent, but
here we have a development of architectural style
which is not found across the channel.

We have to consider forms and characteristics
which are easily, and at once, recognized as belonging
to this particular period and to no other. Before
doing so, let me note a few influences.

In dealing with the latter part of the preceding
period I hinted that a gentle decline had set in. In
this last stage of the Gothic style, although the pro-
fuseness of the earlier periods was carried on abroad
with further exaggeration, here in England the declin-
ing tendency was arrested. A new and delightful
style was slowly but surely evolved. Many fine
churches were built in this period, and not only was
it the result of the religious enthusiasm which prevailed at the time, for it was chiefly due to the
greater power possessed by the democracy—the
middle and working classes—rather than the nobility.

Here, as always, the architecture of a period faith-
fully reflects the history of the people who produced it.

During the six reigns—Richard II, Henry IV, V,

and VI, Edward IV, V, and Richard III—of this period, it was enacted that *every one* should pay taxes, and also that all labourers were now to receive a definite wage. All were made to feel individually responsible for the country's welfare, with position and responsibility, and were thereby given a sense of dignity.

Firstly, then, we shall find that this style was dignified.

Secondly, there was wealth. Good trade was made possible, with a greater security given it by law (which heretofore the middle classes had not enjoyed). There was therefore nothing paltry in this style.

Thirdly, there was an accumulation from down the centuries of fine traditions and the craftsmanship it had produced. Thus the workmanship was of good quality.

So, with these influences at work you will rightly expect to find that the churches of this period were *dignified*, they were *not skimped* in any way, and they were *cleverly constructed*.

Moreover, those sister crafts of painting (whether on glass, stone, or wood) and of wood carving, which were so much a part of the architecture of this period and had so great an influence in the design of its windows and mouldings, flourished exceedingly in this last great effort of the mediaeval builders.

All this was so during the major portion of the period—in fact, until towards the end of the hundred years it covers, when a final and serious decline obtained a hold. The mediaeval art gave way to the drastic changes brought about by the Reformation, a period beyond the scope of this little book. But it died fighting, as it were, for you will find throughout the land examples of this last of the great mediaeval styles built many years after 1485, and its resources do not seem by any means to have been exhausted.

The name Perpendicular is very fairly descriptive, but there is also much about the work which may be described as horizontal. This at first appears a contradiction, but it is not so. The two combined give a squareness. This squareness does not by any means create a plainness ; rather, the repetition of the horizontal line together with, or opposed to, the Perpendicular line forms a *panelled effect* very often spread over the entire building, inside and out. There are cases where there is scarcely a stone in the whole building which is not treated in this way.

BUTTRESSES.—As the wndows were wider the greater was the necessity for deeper buttresses. The

FIG. 112. LOWER BEBINGTON, CHESHIRE

window often takes up the whole of the wall space between these buttresses, and there was practically no wall left, as we see in the example from Lower Bebington (Fig. 112). The buttress projects out from the wall at right angles, but it has a deeper projection than ever, and had often a panelled surface like other parts of the building.

WINDOWS.—The windows are very large and wide, for there was a yet greater demand for stained glass, which is referred to at length in Chapter XIII.

Owing to this greater size, the tracery of which they were composed became important and had to be sufficiently strong to withstand the strong winds which would blow against it. Most of the mullions or the upright bars of the tracery were for this reason carried

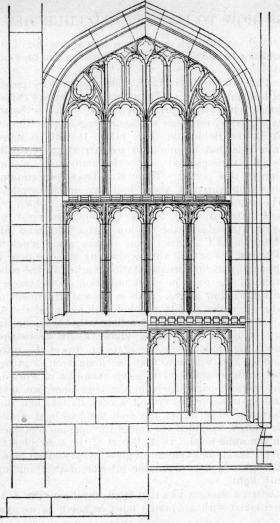

FIG. 113. LOWER BEBINGTON, CHESHIRE

straight up through to the main arch above (Fig. 113), and not twisted and turned as noted in the previous style.

The windows were further strengthened by means of horizontal bars, or TRANSOMES, as they are called, which cross the upright mullions. This is better explained by reference to the drawing of the window at Lower Bebington (Fig. 113). It will be noted from this that the mullions are carried up vertically —right through and up to the main arch—a sure sign of this period. There is a TRANSOME running across horizontally, about half-way up the window. The left-hand side of the sketch (Fig. 113), which is a half external view, shows the buttress right up against the edge of the window. The right-hand side shows a half internal view of the same window. Between the actual window opening and the floor is shown a panelled ornamentation worked in the solid stone of the wall, in exact imitation of the tracery to the window above. This is the wall treatment of which I spoke, and to which I shall again refer. As a cresting to this stone panelling—that is, along the top of it—is a moulding known as an Embattled moulding, and this occurs again on top of the transome. You will note that the main arch is rather flat or depressed, and in some examples of work in this period, particularly in the later ones, we shall find that the arches are often even flatter than this example. The flatter the arch the less light would be wasted, provided the top of the opening remained on the same level. It is all part of the same plan to give a maximum amount of glass, often stained glass, through which to flood the interior of the building with light.

Often a window like that from Barnham (Fig. 114) is covered with a squared label or hood, as we saw occurred occasionally in the last period (Fig. 106), but here the tracery itself is brought up to the square, and also contains a round-headed form, reminding us of the far back Norman round arch. When the mullion is carried through, straight up to the flat

FIG. 114. A SQUARE-HEADED WINDOW FROM BARNHAM, SUSSEX. DATE 1500. SHOWING A PERPENDICULAR PERIOD FORM. PART OF THE TRACERY FORM IS SEMICIRCULAR, GOING BACK TO THE OLD NORMAN ROUND-HEADED FORM

FIG. 115. BARNHAM, SUSSEX. A POINTED DOORWAY UNDER A SQUARED LABEL MOULD-ING. CARVED TRIANGULAR SPANDREL. LATE PERPENDICULAR. 1500

head, it is very typical of the windows of the end of this period.

The fact that the openings sometimes develop into square-headed forms in this style is not without interest. Although we are only dealing with ecclesiastical examples here, we must remember that domestic architecture was developing in parallel. Now, in houses there would be various floors giving horizontal divisions to the design. It very naturally followed that a square-headed window would meet the case far better than a pointed one. This influenced church architecture.

By now more or less peaceful domesticity would be possible, the house architecture would receive more attention, be developed, and the windows made to suit the horizontal floors. The shape having been found a satisfactory one in appearance, its form would be adopted for buildings other than houses.

DOORWAYS.—This idea of squareness spread to the upper parts of the doorways, where we find a square termination formed by mouldings above, which enclose the flat-pointed arch. The sketch from Barnham (Fig. 115) shows a heavy moulding, which is really a Hood mould, because it projects from the face of the wall. Between this and the flat arch of the doorway is a triangular space known as a Spandrel, which in this case is carved with cusped and foliated tracery borrowed from the form used in windows.

You will note that the arch mouldings, very simple in this case, are continued right down to the ground without any intervening cap. This is quite characteristic of the period, although, as we saw, it is found occasionally in the Decorated style.

ARCADES, COLUMNS, AND MOULDINGS.—Turning to the general question of the main internal columns supporting the main arcades, and to the mouldings generally, which always give us distinctive features in all the styles, it will be seen from the sketch from Arundel (Fig. 116) that the main columns or piers, as they are better called, are composed of four part-columns connected by hollows. These hollows are shallow. This lack of depth is typical of all the mouldings in this style.

The *base* of this column or set of part-columns (Figs. 116, 117, 118)—is interesting. It is formed of

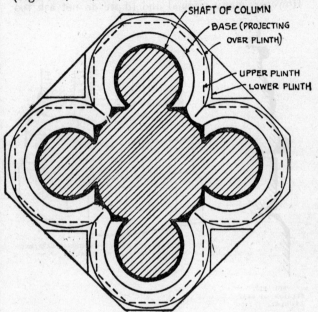

SHAFT OF COLUMN

BASE (PROJECTING OVER PLINTH)

UPPER PLINTH

LOWER PLINTH

FIG. 116. PLAN OF A PIER OR COLUMN FROM ARUNDEL, SUSSEX, ARRANGED IN AN EARLY PERPENDICULAR MANNER. FOUR PART-COLUMNS WITH HOLLOWS BETWEEN. 1380

what may be described as the BRACKET or Double Ogee form of moulding (Fig. 117). Below this is a sub-base or plinth, which is many-sided (Fig. 118). The bases, with their plinths, were made much of in this period.

You may realize the signs of poverty, or I might

say degeneration, if you study the shallowness of the section through the base, as shown at Fig. 117.

There is much loss of the former boldness and character throughout this Perpendicular period. However, many original and (if we do not ask too

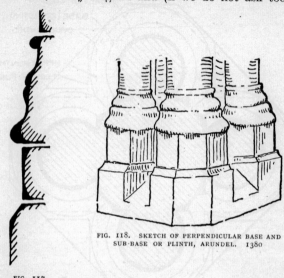

FIG. 118. SKETCH OF PERPENDICULAR BASE AND SUB-BASE OR PLINTH, ARUNDEL. 1380

FIG. 117.
SECTION OF BASE,
ARUNDEL. 1380

closely how and why) striking effects are obtained by a combination of the features which we are now considering, and we must always bear in mind that these mouldings may have been purposely given a flattened form in order to allow the painter a broader surface for his colour schemes.

The section through the arch, as shown in Fig. 119, is again simple and rather shallow.

The caps as here shown (Fig. 120) were often many-sided, that is, they were not circular on plan (looking down) as so often in the Early English style. The example in Fig. 120 has a fair amount of character but many of the examples are plainer.

The plan of the column from St. Olave's (Fig. 121), a London example which escaped the Great Fire in

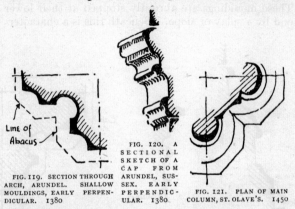

LINE OF
Abacus

FIG. 119. SECTION THROUGH ARCH, ARUNDEL. SHALLOW MOULDINGS, EARLY PERPENDICULAR. 1380

FIG. 120. A SECTIONAL SKETCH OF A CAP FROM ARUNDEL, SUSSEX. EARLY PERPENDICULAR. 1380

FIG. 121. PLAN OF MAIN COLUMN, ST. OLAVE'S. 1450

1666, shows three-quarter columns, divided as before by a shallow moulding of concave form.

The base (Fig. 122) has a little more character than we sometimes find ; there is again the BRACKET mould. It will be noted that the lower part or plinth is octagonal on plan, whilst the upper part of the base is circular.

The cap (Fig. 123) is well moulded and relies for effect upon this breaking up of its surface rather than on any ornament.

The section of the arch of the main arcade (Fig. 124) is composed of characteristically shallow mouldings, but the result is by no means displeasing. Note the central feature, which is known as a casement, i.e. a very shallow hollow.

On reference to the base of the door-jamb from Arundel (Fig. 125) you will see an interesting development. There is no little column in the jamb as previously. A set of shallow mouldings (one is a large casement hollow) forms the side of the doorway. These mouldings are abruptly stopped at their lower end by a splay or slope. Beneath this is a character-

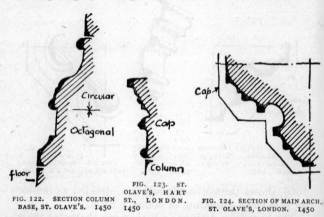

FIG. 122. SECTION COLUMN BASE, ST. OLAVE'S. 1450

FIG. 123. ST. OLAVE'S, HART ST., LONDON. 1450

FIG. 124. SECTION OF MAIN ARCH, ST. OLAVE'S, LONDON. 1450

istic moulding of the period, serving as a kind of base. Moreover, the set of jamb mouldings is carried continuously round the entire doorway (not shown) with no intervening cap. It is quite usual in these doorways, whether square-headed or flat-pointed, to find that the mouldings are carried round with no caps or proper bases. This omission is logical, because mouldings of jamb and arch are similar, but something of the character of earlier periods is here wanting.

ORNAMENT.—There is not a great deal of ornament

to be found in this style other than that in the
vaulting. Apart from the embattled moulding,
which is really a broken moulding and may therefore
be classed as ornament, you will find representations
of certain natural forms, such as the vine, but always
conventionalized and brought into the " squared "
form, to which I referred earlier as being typical of
the style. Heraldic emblems in this style began to
be paramount, and we often find representations in
stone of the Tudor rose and the portcullis.

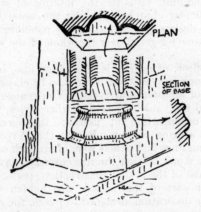

FIG. 125. ARUNDEL CHURCH. BASE OF DOOR JAMB IN THE PERPENDICULAR
PERIOD. THE MOULDINGS WERE OFTEN CARRIED ROUND THE ARCH WITHOUT
ANY CAP. IF ANY BASE, IT WAS INDEPENDENT AS HERE SHOWN. 1380

I am inclined to ask the question, Do we really
miss the ornamental details in this style ? I think
not, for the whole of the church was a mass of wall
surface, broken up with panelled designs, panelled
groined roofs, and large traceried windows—all with
added colour !

VAULTING.—Although vaulting is dealt with in

another chapter it will be as well to say a general word here under this heading.

Its design is in keeping with the rest of the church in two respects. Firstly, its arch form is of the flattened type, apart from added ornament ; was a flattened arch ; it was not pointed but of a continuous curve, like a flattened out Norman barrel vault. Secondly, its surface is composed of a network of panelling of similar design to the panelling on the walls or the tracery of the windows. We might well, therefore, visualize the interior of a vaulted Perpendicular church by taking the usual traceried window design and repeating its panelling (substituting stone for glass) over the whole of the walls and ceiling.

The effect, of course, is often very fine, but there is too much falsity about it for it to be classed as the highest of architectural types. You remember that we found the vaulting ribs, in earlier styles, were not merely ornamental but useful ; they were main arches, carrying weight. But in the Perpendicular style mouldings and panels were often both carved on the same stone, so that the ribs ceased to have meaning. Most of the actual construction, particularly in the later part of this period, was hidden away by elaborate decoration, designed to puzzle the observer.

SUMMARY

PERPENDICULAR

1. WALLS.—What there is left of wall surfaces, after allowing for very wide windows with buttresses between, is treated with stone

panelled work (copied from the window tracery).

2. BUTTRESSES.—Very deep and important.

3. WINDOWS.—Very wide. Flat- (or blunt-) pointed arched openings or square-headed openings. Distinctive tracery. Mullions carried up to the arch, and transomes across the window.

4. DOORWAYS.—Flat-pointed arched openings, or square-headed with carved spandrels.

5. ARCADES AND COLUMNS.—Four half or three-quarter columns connected by shallow concave mouldings.

6. CAPS.—These do not always exist. Sometimes round, sometimes many-sided on plan. Moulded. The abacus and bell together form one series of mouldings.

7. BASES.—Important. Bracket-moulded. Often resting on a sub-base or plinth.

8. MOULDINGS.—Wide and shallow. Casement bracket, embattled. Ogee.

9. ORNAMENT.—Not much used except in the vaulting. Tudor rose and portcullis, and other heraldic symbols.

CHAPTER VIII

GENERAL ARRANGEMENT OF A
TYPICAL CHURCH

I HERE show (Fig. 126) a fully-developed church. It is typical of any of the periods to which I have referred, except that in the earlier or later periods the shape of the vaulting or the shape of the arches would vary. The disposition and not the actual shape of the parts is the matter now under immediate consideration. All that I say of large churches is equally true of cathedrals; for these latter are merely churches which contain the seat of a bishop, and are therefore necessarily large and important.

The first view shows an interior. Starting near the ground, we note clustered columns, supporting pointed arches; these form the nave arcade. Just above is a row of openings, resembling windows, but not filled in with glass. These do not connect with the outside of the building, for beyond them is merely the space over the aisle roof. This middle division of the side of a church which we are now considering is known as a Blind Story, for the window-like openings admit no light. It is also known as a Triforium. I show it to illustrate the complete scheme, though in a parish church mere plain wall or panelling takes its place.

Above this, the uppermost division of the side of our building, is the Clerestory, so named because in this case it does admit light (from French *clair*, meaning light), and is, in fact, the chief source of light to the Nave or body of the church. An example of a clerestory window from a small church is shown from Arundel (Fig. 127). You will also see above this, how the ribs of the stone ceiling or vaulting carry the weight of the ceiling down to certain points

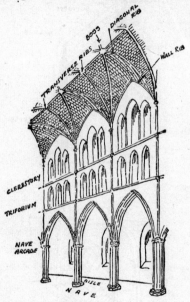

FIG. 126. SIMPLIFIED OUTLINE OF A TYPICAL CATHEDRAL OR MONASTIC CHURCH

on the wall; these points will be found, if you will refer to Fig. 126A (which is a section through the same kind of building, just as if you were to cut a slice out of it in a downward direction) just where the buttresses occur.

A flying buttress is an arch crossing over an open

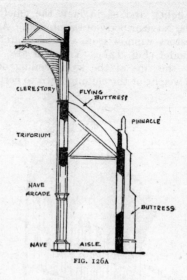

CLERESTORY · FLYING BUTTRESS

PINNACLE

TRIFORIUM

NAVE ARCADE

BUTTRESS

NAVE · AISLE.

FIG. 126A

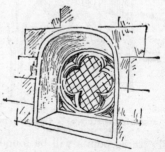

FIG. 127. CLERESTORY WINDOW, ARUNDEL. A CLERESTORY WINDOW
OCCURS ABOVE THE ARCHES OF THE MAIN NAVE ARCADE

space connecting the upper part of the side of a nave wall with an ordinary buttress on the aisle wall. These buttresses are taking the weight from the stone roofs. I will explain this more fully, for it is an outstanding feature of Gothic construction, the like of which would not be found in Classic architecture.

In any arch construction resting on walls, as in the example of vaulting before us, there is a decided tendency for the arch form to push the walls outwards.

You will easily understand this by a simple experiment. Place two matchboxes on the table, a few inches apart ; now bend over a fairly stiff piece of paper into arch form, so that the lower part of the arched paper rests on the table, between and against the boxes. Now if you will exert a little pressure on the top of the paper arch the boxes will slide outwards. This pressure represents the weight of the stone vaulting, and the boxes are the buttresses, which, if they were sufficiently heavy, would withstand the pressure and nothing would move. The Gothic buttress thus prevents the walls being pushed out by the vaulting.

Every stone in a Gothic building is always *about* to move, but is prevented by the one next to it, and so on, until the ground is reached. Take one of the matchboxes away and the paper arch will collapse, for the other box is no good by itself. That is one reason why, when a Gothic building once commences to decay and break up, the weakness spreads very quickly, and the whole building is soon in ruins. There is little left of it above the ground, unless the first defects are made good at once. On the other hand, you will find, when you study Classic architecture, that you would be able to take away part of the Classic building, without the remainder collapsing.

There are many Classic ruins but few Gothic ones. There have been many instances where examples of both styles of buildings have been partly destroyed, say in times of war, and each partially wrecked. If the Gothic example has not been immediately restored, it has gone, but not so the Classic one ; its few columns, with beams resting on them, are there to this day, and will not disappear until another war or some such catastrophe occurs. To explain the Classic principle we take our two matchboxes and stand them on end, for columns ; across these we *rest* a flat ruler to represent a beam. There is here no tendency for anything to move in any direction.

The Greeks—the greatest exponents of Classic Art —had no use for the restless arch : they put beams across columns and it was finished. The Gothic builders, from their lack of big stones to go right across, took many small stones and built an arch, with its tendency to move, then imprisoned it within the buttresses.

So we see now how the buttresses take the weight of the vaulting in a Gothic building. If the building be a low one an ordinary buttress suffices ; if high, a flying buttress is necessary in addition, and sometimes, in the latter case, the ordinary buttress is terminated at its upper end by a turret-like pinnacle. The stabilizing effect of this pinnacle can be proved by adding extra weights to the matchboxes of our experiment.

PLAN.—As regards the plan of a church, or, as I might say, the arrangement of its various parts in relation to the ground, I have already hinted as to how a church may commence with just a nave, with a chancel leading out of it towards the east, and how aisles would be the next development, and so on.

I here show (Fig. 128) a fully-developed plan quite

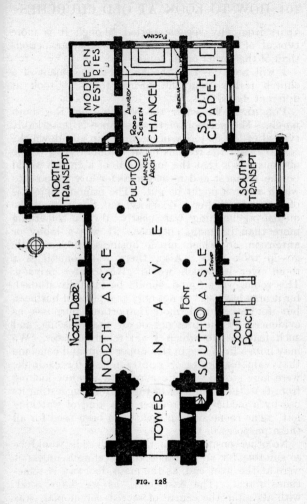

PISCINA

MODERN VESTRIES

ROOD SCREEN

AUMBRY

CHANCEL

SEDILIA

SOUTH CHAPEL

NORTH TRANSEPT

PULPIT

CHANCEL ARCH

SOUTH TRANSEPT

N A V E

NORTH AISLE

NORTH DOOR

SOUTH AISLE

STOUP

FONT

SOUTH PORCH

TOWER

FIG. 128

apart from any specific period, though it is more typical of the Decorated or Perpendicular periods than of the earlier ones.

I will now describe the general arrangement of a church rather than the special forms it took at different dates.

PORCHES.—We enter the church from the south porch. The position of this entrance is remarkably typical of the majority of churches up and down the country, and the reasons for it are interesting. The obvious one is that the south side of a church would be the warmest and most genial for any purpose to which a porch might be put. The primary object is of course to shelter a doorway, but this part of the mediaeval building was nearly always something more than its main entrance. It was a lobby or ante-room in which much business and no little gossip took place. Also, there was sometimes a room over it, which would give greater privacy. This room, when found, should be carefully studied, for it may have served not only as a place of business, but for other and more important purposes as evidenced by the presence of an altar, piscina, and such features, to which I am referring later. We may note a fire-place in this upper room and conclude that valuable books or saintly relics, for example, were here stored. There may be a window looking from it to the main part of the church, suggesting its use by a mediaeval caretaker as a kind of watching loft. The room may, in fact, have been used for all these purposes in turn.

No other position than this south side would be so suitable for an entrance to the church unless it were at the west end, as the main doorway is some-times found. The east end, as we have said with its altar the centre of sacred ceremonial, was specially reserved for the clergy, and not the general public.

What of the north side ? Why was this not generally used ? Largely because it has a special significance, and I shall refer again to this under the paragraph dealing with the North Door.

This south porch, then, is important and therefore built in a substantial manner. It would be of stone, if there was stone available, and its design will give us a clue as to its date. If the church was not in a good stone district, the porch is the portion of the building which could, if necessary, be built in timber, or at any rate, partly in timber. The latter type is mentioned later when dealing with other woodwork. In whatever material it was built we shall expect to find these important adjuncts to the church, comfortable sheltered places, provided with benches on which all and sundry could rest and talk.

Let me continue my notes on doorways, for there are two other interesting ones often, but not always, found.

NORTH DOOR.—Cross over to the other side of the church, opposite the south door. If you should find the main entrance to the church on the north side, you will probably also find that a manor house or part of the village is also in that position. In many instances, however, there will be found a less important doorway on the north side of a church, which has been filled in. The form of the doorway, with its mouldings, is still there, but the actual door has been replaced by masonry. Its former use is somewhat conjectural, but certainly worth inquiry. It is, for one thing, nearly always small and comparatively unimportant, and one may therefore conclude that it was only occasionally used. Owing to the belief, attributed to mediaeval worshippers, that the Evil One constantly tried to exert influence from this direction—a belief which is shown in the fact that unbaptized and excommunicated persons were buried on this unfavoured side of the church—it has come to be known as the " Devil's Door." It probably served for the priest or the occupant of an adjacent manor.

The same belief is reflected in the fact that those ugly gargoyles we see at the corners near the roof outside have been thought to represent the Devil degraded to the menial task of carrying away the rain water.

However this may be, when these uses no longer existed the doorway would be walled up, as we see it to-day.

The third interesting doorway is found towards the east end, viz.,

THE PRIEST'S OR SANCTUARY DOOR.—You will occasionally meet with a small door on the south side —again the usual side of approach—but this time on the chancel wall. It was probably used as a private means of approach by the priest, though it has been suggested that it was used by those fleeing from justice and seeking sanctuary in those early times when privileged right of asylum was sometimes granted to the Church.

Having dealt with the doorways, I will now return to the plan under review.

TOWER.—This is commonly found at the west end, as shown in the typical plan, and there is usually a doorway on its west side forming the west entrance to the church, and except in very early times an important and imposing arch occurred between the west tower and the nave. This entrance to the church would have special significance as it would lend itself well to the purpose of processions. The tower may, of course, be found elsewhere, such as at the crossing (where the nave is crossed by the transepts). In many cases at the corner of the tower is a little staircase, built in the wall, for access to the floor above, usually the " ringing chamber," from whence the bells might be rung.

NAVE, AISLES, CHANCEL, ETC.—In the typical plan we are considering there is an aisle on the north side of the nave and another on the south. These aisles are divided from the nave by arcades, each consisting in this case of four arches.

The crossing gives on to transepts, one on the north side and one on the south.

Near the pulpit, which is in the crossing, is a staircase which led at one time to a rood-loft, about which, and the rood-screen hereabouts, I shall have more to say later.

Passing into the chancel with its altar at the east end, on the north side of the chancel is a doorway leading to the choir vestry and eventually to the clergy vestry (both almost certain to be of modern erection). You will note that the wall on the south side of the chancel has been broken away and an arcade formed in its place. Within the arcade is a screen shutting off a chapel. This chapel has an altar of its own. Indeed, there may be several chapels within the one church, dedicated to various saints ; but these may be chantry chapels, in which case they would be of no little interest.

CHANTRY CHAPELS.—Throughout the history of man there have always been individuals—people of prosperity and standing—who have, as a token of their religious fervour, given of their wealth to the Church.

In Saxon times churches were erected by religious communities or by individuals, and individual generosity was responsible for much similar building in Norman times. In fact, a very great number of churches were erected in that period. But, in the EARLY ENGLISH and later mediaeval times, when there were already plenty of churches, an interesting development occurred. What happened was this.

It was by no means uncommon for a public bene-factor—anyone of means—to set aside or bequeath or make an endowment of money or lands for the benefit of priests. These priests in return would have to say Mass, to pray for the donor's welfare in life, or soul in death.

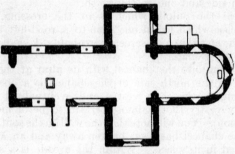

FIG. 129. WORTH

These services took place in an existing part of the church, or in an extension of the church specially erected for this purpose, adjacent to what was perhaps a much earlier church. This endowment or gift is known as a Chantry, the priests as Chantry Priests and the portion of the building where the services were held the Chantry Chapel.

Thus we shall find many instances where the development of the plan of a church took the form of an extra chapel with its own altar. For example, in an Early English church the adaptation or extension might well be in the Decorated or Perpendicular style. Again, an Early English transept may be screened off by a Perpendicular screen.

APSE.—You will occasionally meet with an east end of a church which is not square but round, known as an Apse, as shown on the plan of Worth (Fig. 129), a rare example of a Saxon apse.

When this arrangement is found it rather suggests a Norman plan, or, if of later date, that there was some foreign influence at work, for the apse was almost universal on the Continent.

These apsidal terminations, as they are called, are found in a few English cathedrals, but the difficulty of construction and consequent greater cost would not make this form popular with builders responsible for the smaller churches, and so in this country the square east end prevailed.

FIG. 129A.   PLAN OF EARLY SAXON CHURCH, ESCOMB

CHAPTER IX

ROOFS AND VAULTING

WE have spoken of stone ceilings and of their importance in regard to the evolution of the pointed arch; but it is necessary to note that each building would have a timber roof, although not every timber roof would be protected inside by a stone ceiling or "vaults."

FIG. 130. HEXHAM. GROINED VAULTING WITH MOULDED RIBS

Before passing on to the consideration of timber roofs it will be as well to state briefly what we may expect to find as characteristic of each period in the matter of stone ceilings.

VAULTING AND STONE CEILINGS.—In each of the three Gothic styles, Early English, Decorated, and

Perpendicular, the vaulting was of pointed arches. The pointedness became flatter as time went on, until in the last period—the Perpendicular—it was very flat. In all cases there are ribs, that is, a framework of stone, with a thin curved or arched web of stonework in between the ribs.

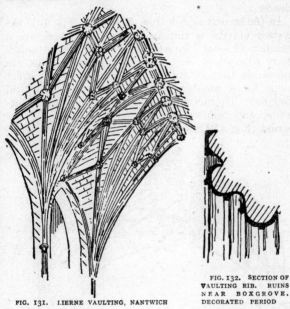

FIG. 131. LIERNE VAULTING, NANTWICH

FIG. 132. SECTION OF VAULTING RIB. RUINS NEAR BOXGROVE. DECORATED PERIOD

The three sketches—Figs. 130, 131, and 133—show something of the development of vaulting in stone.

In the first sketch from Hexham (Fig. 130), which is an Early English example of vaulting, it will be seen that the idea is a simple framework of moulded ribs. The ribs meet each other, across from side to side and diagonally from corner to corner, and meet at the top. This meeting point is known as the APEX, and the continuous top of the vaulting usually on the one level is called the RIDGE.

The sketch previously given of the typical interior (Fig. 126) will make this method of construction clearer.

In the second sketch from Nantwich (Fig. 131) the system of ribs is similar, except that there are a number of *short* intermediate ribs. These subsidiary ribs, which branch off from the main ribs, are known as LIERNE Ribs. This method allows great scope for a number of very varied and beautiful designs. The actual moulding of the ribs is interesting and follows in each style the type of the period (Fig. 132, Boxgrove), with its filleted rolls.

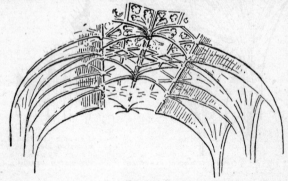

FIG. 133

The Perpendicular example (Fig. 133) shows—at the side—a kind of FAN vaulting, which spreads out and supports, or appears to support, a flat ceiling. The flat ceiling, however, is relieved by horizontal ribs. In the centre of the vault are PENDANTS, or portions hanging down, in a decidedly mysterious way.

The rich effect produced by some of these overhanging and pendent masses of heavy stonework is truly marvellous.

There is, however, only one simple principle of construction to explain in order to get behind its mystery. It is the principle of the KEYSTONE. A keystone is the main centre stone of any arch, which by reason of its shape being that of a wedge cannot fall. There is no reason at all why this keystone should not be a long stone and project well below the main arch and be an elaborately shaped stone, which from its lower end supports little miniature vaults, and this is just what it does do.

The point of deception is that the upper part of the wedge-shaped keystone and the main arch of which it forms the centre stone are hidden from view by the little subsidiary vaults which the lower end of the long keystone supports.

I will explain it in this way. Place your two hands slanting upwards, so that the finger-tips of the one hand touch the finger-tips of the other. This will represent the main vault. Now place the top end of a short pencil between the tops of the two first fingers and let the pencil hang downwards. This will represent a long keystone, held only at its upper end. Now imagine the bottom of the pencil to be thickened out and shaped and carved, and from this carved lower end imagine arched vaulting curving back to, say, half-way up the inside of your fingers.

By keeping the finger-tips together it would be possible to support a considerable weight.

This is what happens in a roof with pendants, but you only see the underside of the pendants and the subsidiary vaulting.

I

TIMBER ROOFS.—The open timber roofs are in
many instances beautiful and certainly varied.

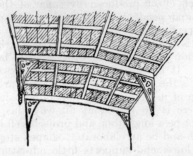

FIG. 134. ROOF, ARUNDEL. SHOWING CAMBERED TIE-BEAMS WITH
FOLIATED BRACKETS. THE PURLINS AND RAFTERS ABOVE GIVE A PANELLED
EFFECT

FIG. 135. LYMINSTER, SUSSEX. AISLE ROOF SHOWING CAMBERED TIE-BEAM
WITH STRUTS BELOW AND KING-POST ABOVE

There may be only a simple beam fixed across from
wall to wall. These beams would probably be, say,

ten feet apart. That is, every ten feet along the nave for example there would be a beam.

This is known as a TIE BEAM (Fig. 136), for it ties in the walls, which might otherwise be pushed out by the " rafters," or sloping pieces forming the actual roof. There may be an upright post from the tie

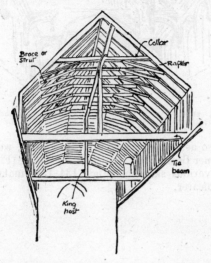

FIG. 136. ICKENHAM, MIDDLESEX. ROOF, SHOWING TIE-BEAM, KING-POST

beam, known as a King Post (Fig. 136). These king posts are often moulded.

When the rafters are long, as they necessarily would be in a fairly wide nave, they need tying in with Collars about half-way up the roof (Fig. 136). These rafters may also be connected together by Braces or Struts further to strengthen the framework (Fig. 136). The braces may be curved. If there is a

bracket formation out from each wall under the ends
of the tie beam and the tie beam is cut away in its

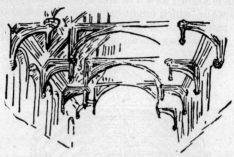

FIG. 137.   ELTHAM PALACE, 1482, SHOWING A HAMMER-BEAM ROOF, WHERE
THE WEIGHT OF THE ROOF IS BROUGHT DOWN BELOW THE TOP OF THE WALL

centre so as to have mere projecting ends, we call it
a Hammer Beam Roof, as at Eltham Palace (Fig. 137).

The various sketches (Figs. 134–137) make these
points clearer.

CHAPTER X

FONT, STOUP, PISCINA

THESE three items of church furniture are connected with Holy Water.

The Font should be looked for at the west end of the church, probably near the south doorway or at any rate near the main entrance. The Saxon and all

FIG. 138. FONT, BOSHAM. THE UPPER PART, OR BOWL, IS SIX-SIDED AND RESTS ON THE LARGE SHAFT AND FOUR SMALLER ONES

other periods are represented by examples. Their various forms make an interesting study, for, in each case we shall find that the general characteristics of the style are followed.

They may be round, six- or eight-sided.

The early carvers often put the best they knew

into their fonts (see a Norman example as Fig. 139), but sometimes a font is a plain square basin, perhaps a tub shape on a pillar (both Norman types). Early English often rest on clustered columns. Decorated ones are richly ornamented.

Perpendicular fonts (Fig. 140) were usually eight-sided and richly panelled.

The example shown from Bosham (Fig. 138) probably of two dates. The upper part is of simple

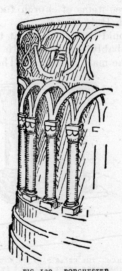

FIG. 139. PORCHESTER

design in a hard material, marble ; it looks earlier in design than the supports, which appear to be Early English. But it may be borne in mind that a design worked on a hard material would probably be simple in any period.

The covers should be looked for, as they are often

very elaborate examples of the wood-carver's art, especially in the later periods.

Fonts would make an interesting study in which to specialize, for there is always one to be found in every church, and no two quite alike.

STOUP.—A stoup which served in mediaeval times as a receptacle for holy water for the use of laymen must be looked for in the porch, generally the south porch, or inside the church near the main entrance.

It is a vessel formed in a little recess in the wall with usually a little moulded roof over. The mouldings and general treatment will be the key to its date.

PISCINA.—A piscina at first appears to be similar to a stoup, but it was used for a different purpose. There is a hole in the bottom forming a drain for the water which had been used by the priest when washing his hands and the sacred vessels. Sometimes it was of a double form, with two drains. It will be found near, generally south of, the site of an altar, either the high altar or at the end of one of the aisles, when it shows that there was at one time, if not to-day, an altar near by. The altar may have been removed, but not necessarily the basin and drain forming the piscina.

FIG. 140.   PERPENDICULAR FONT, CONWAY

CHAPTER XI

SEATING: BENCHES, SEDILIA, MISERICORD. AUMBRY, EASTER SEPULCHRE, SQUINT, LOWSIDE WINDOW

MEDIAEVAL woodworkers exhibited great skill in the pews and benches. Many of the bench-ends were carved in what is known as the POPPY-HEAD design, such as the example I show at Sefton (Fig. 141).

In the nave rough wooden benches were used from early times, but most of the examples are of the later periods. There were usually stone benches around the walls and around the pillars of the main nave arcade where many of the worshippers could sit.

SEDILE, OR SEDILIA.—This is the name given to a seat or seats used by the clergy whilst celebrating Mass, generally consisting of elaborately carved stone recesses, with canopies over, and situated on the south wall of the chancel near the high altar. The date of these will be recognized from the general formation and detail of the carving, and are nearly always extremely beautiful. There may be any number of recesses up to five side by side.

A MISERICORD is a wooden seat so hinged at its back edge that when it is tipped up a ledge projects which affords a certain amount of rest when a person is standing and leaning back upon it. The space beneath the ledge, visible when the seat is tipped up, is always well carved. These are often found in the choir stalls of cathedrals or important churches when there was a connexion between the church and one or other of the cathedrals.

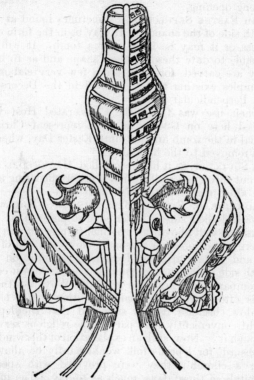

FIG. 141.   A CARVED POPPY-HEAD FROM SEFTON, LANCS., BEING THE UPPER PART OF THE END OF A PEW CARVED IN WOOD

An AUMBRY, which is a cupboard in the wall for sacred vessels, may often be found at the north side of the chancel near the high altar.

It may have lost its wooden doors, in which case it would now show only a recess in the wall, and is not necessarily an elaborate affair, but usually a plain oblong opening.

An EASTER SEPULCHRE is sometimes found at the north side of the chancel. It may be in the form of a recess or it may be in or near a tomb. It will be possible to date these by their shape and as to how they are carved, for there are a few very elaborate examples existing to-day, erected in the Decorated and Perpendicular styles.

Their use was this: the Consecrated Host was placed here on Good Friday to represent Christ's burial in the tomb and left until Easter Day, when it was removed to the high altar.

A SQUINT or, as it has been called, HAGIOSCOPE is a slit cut through a wall so that a priest officiating at a side altar might see the high altar.

LOWSIDE, OR SANCTUS-BELL WINDOW.—Most windows had their sills or lower edge so placed that the glass was well above the eye-line, to prevent thieves entering and for other reasons. Now, you will often see and wonder at a small window, generally on the south side of the chancel, built so that its lowest edge is comparatively near the ground. Why was this? It is often erroneously said that this was a leper window, because it was supposed that the lepers might conveniently take part in the religious service through it! Now, such an explanation of this window is absurd, for leprous folk would hardly be allowed near a church; they were provided with special hospitals in those days, much as to-day. The more reasonable suggestion to accept is this: When the officiating priest reached certain solemn moments of the daily service a server rang a sanctus-bell—a hand-bell rung through the window—to inform all who might hear that the sacred rites were at that moment being celebrated within their church. Look for a wooden shutter or the remains (hinges) of one.

ALMSBOX.—A few ancient oak examples remain, with their early locks, and are worthy of study ; and perhaps I may appropriately remind you that if there is a box for contributions to the renovation fund, we who have been interested should not let the opportunity pass of showing some practical appreciation.

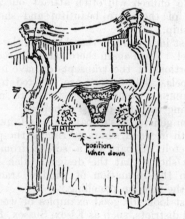

FIG. 141A. STALL WITH HINGED SEAT (MISERICORD), NORTH WALSHAM

CHAPTER XII

SCREENS, WOODEN PORCHES, AND ROOD-LOFTS

THE screens or wooden divisions in various parts of the church will often attract our attention, for many of them are beautiful and show skilful workmanship.

The most important is that between the nave and the chancel. Then again there may be screens dividing off portions of the transepts or nave in order to form chapels. The former are referred to later as ROOD-SCREENS, whilst the latter were mentioned when dealing with the chantry chapels.

The form generally is of panelling and open tracery above, both in wood, characteristic of the period.

The sketch of part of a screen from Huyton (Fig. 142) shows that the designs which had been evolved in the formation of window tracery were copied in the wooden panelling.

We must look for good examples of woodcarving in wooded districts, such as Essex, Sussex, Kent, and Cheshire, as well as in the wooded parts of other counties, e.g. south-west of England.

I show a timber PORCH from Margaretting in Essex (Fig. 143). There are many such throughout the land, mostly of the Decorated or Perpendicular periods. Although this woodwork followed the general characteristics of the period in which it was executed, it must be well borne in mind that certain forms and designs were longer retained in woodwork than in stonework. The change from one style to another took place first in stone then in wood.

FIG. 142. FLOWING TRACERY IN WOOD PANEL IN SCREEN, HUYTON, LANCS.

ROOD-LOFTS.—In every church a particular interest always centres around the chancel arch, or, if there is no arch, the division between the nave and chancel. Every church, as we have already noticed, is divided into two main parts, the nave for the congregation and the chancel for the clergy. The division between the two parts is normally definitely marked by a chancel arch, together with a chancel screen and various other features under the arch or adjoining it.

The Saxon word Rood means a Cross or Crucifix, sometimes used to denote the actual image of Christ. The rood-loft, with which we are now particularly concerned, was put either over the chancel screen —known therefore as a Rood-screen—or thereabouts.

FIG. 143. TIMBER PORCH, MARGARETTING, ESSEX. EARLY PERPENDICULAR PERIOD. THE CHANGE FROM ONE STYLE TO ANOTHER WAS SLOWER IN WOODWORK THAN IN STONEWORK

The ROOD itself may have been either of stone, silver, wood or in the form of a wall painting, and would often be found accompanied on each side by the images of the Virgin Mary and St. John.

In any church but a small one it would be necessary to raise up these images for all to see (except during

Lent, when they were purposely veiled). This was done by placing the images upon a ROOD-BEAM across the chancel arch above the screen, or in some other suitable place near by.

It is necessary to speak of the ROOD in the past tense, for they were all ordered to be taken down in 1547.

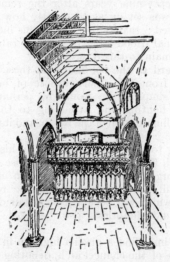

FIG. 144. ROOD-LOFT WITH ROOD-SCREEN BELOW ; ROOD-BEAM AND ROOD
ABOVE ; ROOD STAIRS AT SIDE ; ROOD WINDOW HIGH UP AT SIDE

The ROOD-BEAM may be found in conjunction with a rood-screen below, and a rood-loft above.

The rood-loft, according to the use to which it was put, would require access stairs, which now often remain, at the side, probably right in the thickness of the wall adjoining (Fig. 144).

We shall often find remains of features which

strongly suggest that there was at one time a rood-loft ; so the question as to how these were formed becomes extremely interesting, and the reader may well devote time to collecting data from the various churches and so reconstruct in his imagination exactly what the arrangement was around the chancel arch in mediaeval times.

Some twenty-nine years after the removal order an inquiry was set up as to exactly how much was to be removed ; thanks perhaps to this inquiry some of the original Rood-lofts, or at any rate portions of them, remain to this day.

With regard to the use to which these lofts were put, apart from the chief purpose of holding the ROOD, the simplest use would be perhaps for the purpose of lighting and attending to the candles, used in the illumination of the ROOD, and its attendent figures.

According to Hamilton Thompson in his " Growth of the Parish Church " the " habitual use of the loft was as an organ gallery and the screen at Newark-on-Trent still has at its east side the rectangular projection, which was occupied by a pair of organs."

They would doubtless also be used for vocal purposes.

We sometimes find a piscina high up in the north or south side of the chancel arch, denoting that there was at one time an altar in the rood-loft. The loft would have to be rather wide for this purpose.

A chantry, to which I have already referred, was founded in 1349 in the large stone rood-screen at Grantham (Thompson).

At the present time we may, on examining a church, find little to suggest that a rood-loft ever existed, but it is worth while to examine the masonry, on both sides of the chancel arch, to see whether there is a blocked-up opening ; in fact, the opening itself may be there, or even a few steps now leading nowhere.

On looking up at the underside of the chancel arch we may note the built-in ends of a former rood-beam, sawn off flush with the masonry. Or again there may be hooks for the Lenten veil. A piscina high up in the wall may be looked for.

If the rood-beam remain, the upper surface should be examined for slots or mortices, one central and one on either side for the images. Cross beams may have been notched on to this beam, in which case they would have formed a rood-loft floor, but in that case the rood-beam proper would probably have been a separate beam well above the rood-loft.

Again, there may have been a double screen with a space between forming a wide rood-loft over.

Sometimes the easternmost arch of the nave arcade is unsymmetrical (Fig. 144), or appears to be cut away, and the eastern half of the arch is higher than the western half of the arch. Then the higher springing in the eastern side allowed head-room for a rood-loft.

Not only in the matter of rood-lofts will theories as to the actual arrangement of a church in mediaeval times crowd into your mind as you wander with a seeing eye around any of our glorious old churches, but in many other ways, as when you come across, say, an odd door or window which now no longer retains a use but only a forgotten meaning.

For example, was there, in mediaeval times an upper floor to a church ? You will often note a doorway high up above the ground floor now leading nowhere ; again, there are often to be found stairs or remains of stairs, sometimes three in the one church—one to an upper floor to the tower, one to

K

a room over the porch, and one to the rood-loft—to say nothing of the many wooden stairs to galleries now gone. Was the rood elevated to bring it on to a level with an upper floor over the nave? Then some of the high-up doorways will have their use explained. We see remains of gallery beams, or chases, cut in the columns, high up, which would once receive the ends of such beams.

Again, we know that the chancel at Compton in Surrey was of two stories.

These are merely suggestions to show the kind of interesting problems which will present themselves to the observant.

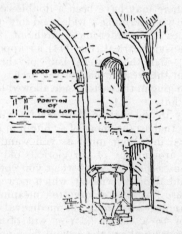

FIG. 144A. DOORS OF ROOD-STAIR TO LOFT, OVERSTRAND

CHAPTER XIII

PAINTINGS, STAINED AND PAINTED GLASS

THE interior of the mediaeval church was, in the majority of cases, a blaze of colour.

The walls, columns, arches, mouldings, roofs, and screens were covered by brightly coloured designs, executed in reds, yellows, blues, greens, and browns. Although there was often delicate beauty in these coloured pictures there was no art for art's sake as in modern times. These pictures were painted in order to teach the people a lesson—to tell them a story and to point a moral. Their success lay in their direct and clear appeal—that was their only object.

We have seen something of the beauty of FORM, as evidenced in the work of the mediaeval stoneworkers, but I will now ask you to imagine this stonework clothed with COLOUR. You will then begin to realize more truly something of the splendour of mediaeval times.

Even this is not enough for a full appreciation of a church in the Middle Ages. Imagine, further, every piece of glass in those windows a part of a coloured picture through which the sun blazes its message to the wondering folk within. You will then possibly catch the spirit of the old-time enthusiasm for religion—a religion which was very much more a part of the people's lives than it is to-day.

The story was told in coloured picture form on walls and in windows, in such a manner that the most ignorant could learn in no uncertain manner the Story of Christianity.

There were several reasons why this form of teaching was the only way in which to bring home to the people the doings of the past and the hopes and fears of the future. First, preaching from the pulpit was not so essential a feature of the ministrations of the Church as now, except by the religious community called the Preaching Friars, who did most of their teaching outside the churches whilst travelling about and not under the auspices of the parish priests. Secondly, there were few books and fewer people able to understand them. Thirdly, the people in the nave would hear the priests in the chancel chanting the services, but the layman would understand but little, if any, of what was going on behind the chancel screen, the clergy using only the Latin language.

Much of this colour work has been wantonly destroyed, some has faded away, whilst in other instances it has been whitewashed over. By no means is all the destruction and whitewashing due to the plundering Reformers of the sixteenth century or the havoc wrought by the Parliamentarians of the seventeenth century, for we must blame with these the so-called " Restorers " of the nineteenth century. These last were apparently not so enlightened as they are to-day.

There is now no excuse for any destruction. If any repairs are undertaken to-day care should be exercised in the removal even of whitewash so as to ascertain whether or not paintings exist beneath.

Textbooks on archæology usually refer to this colour question under the two headings, WALL

PAINTINGS and STAINED AND PAINTED GLASS. Whilst the latter is correct it is misleading to lump together all other paintings as wall paintings; for, although much of the colour work is found on the walls, examples occur on every other part of the interior of the church. We may well, therefore, divide our subject thus: PAINTINGS ON PLASTER, STONE, and WOOD, AND STAINED AND PAINTED GLASS.

Before going into the question of the varying characteristics found in these paintings to enable us to give a date to examples, I will briefly refer to the subjects themselves, which are found in all periods. There may be one exception to this universal application in all periods, that of St. Christopher, which is generally thought never to be much earlier than the Perpendicular period.

SUBJECTS.—The whole range of subjects depicted in these paintings covers the ground from the Creation at the beginning of the world to the Day of Judgment.

Whilst this is not the place to give a complete list I will note a few examples:

The Creation and the story of Adam and Eve begin the series.

The story of Christ begins with the representation of St. Anne, the mother of Mary, and follows on with the life of Mary, the Mother of Jesus. Then the Birth of Our Saviour; Christ with the Doctors in the Temple; the Transfiguration; His Triumphal Entry into Jerusalem; His Agony in the Garden; the Judgment of Pontius Pilate. Then the Crucifixion; the Taking Down from the Cross; the Entombment; and the Resurrection; His Ascension into Heaven; and finally the Descent of the Holy Ghost upon the Apostles.

Further, the Twelve Apostles, the Four Evangelists, the Saints and Martyrs, and even such less worthy characters as Herod, Judas, and others will be found depicted.

Whilst the representation of Our Lord will be easily recognizable it may be as well to give a few emblems, objects or symbols relating to other subjects in alphabetical order, so that reference from a picture or window to this list will facilitate the naming of the subject. I can, of course, only give the saints most frequently associated with the symbols ; there are many others (less often) represented with these emblems.

Anchor.—St. Nicholas and other saints.
Angel.—St. Matthew (one of the four Evangelists).
Axe.—St. Matthew.
Balls (Three Golden).—St. Nicholas.
Basket of Bread.—St. Philip.
Book.—St. Matthew or St. Thomas.
Book in Hand.—St. Anne (Mother of Blessed Virgin) and other saints.
Builder's Rule.—St. Thomas.
Carpenter's Square.—St. Jude and others.
Catherine Wheel.—St. Catherine.
Chalice.—St. John (one of the Evangelists) and other saints.
Dragon.—St. Margaret, St. Michael, and others.
Eagle.—St. John.
Fish.—St. Simon, St. Andrew, and others.
Keys (of Heaven).—St. Peter.
Knife.—St. Bartholomew.
Lamb and Banner.—St. John the Baptist, or St. Agnes.
Lion.—St. Mark (one of the Four Evangelists) and other saints.
Money Box.—St. Matthew.
Napkin.—St. Stephen.

Ox.—St. Luke (one of the Four Evangelists).

Saw.—St. Simon.

Scales.—St. Michael.

Scallop Shell.—St. James.

Shell.—St. James.

Spear.—St. Matthew. If in mouth of Dragon, St. Margaret.

Staff.—St. James or St. Philip, or, if with figure of Christ on shoulder, St. Christopher.

Stone.—St. Stephen.

Sword.—St. Paul, St. Catherine, and other saints.

Tower.—St. Barbara.

Vase of Ointment.—St. Mary Magdalene.

Wallet.—St. John the Evangelist.

PAINTINGS ON PLASTER, STONE, AND WOOD

It is by no means easy to date the numerous examples which you will find; some are so fragmentary. But after you have made notes as to design and colour of all that you come across, you will soon be able to obtain a very fair idea as to the various types.

You may take it as a general rule that all stonework which was shaped into arches, columns, windows, and doorways, that is, all masonry which has a smooth or " worked " surface, was, in the majority of cases, coloured. But what of the rougher stonework forming the main walls around and above openings ? This, especially in the earlier mediaeval times, was purposely left fairly rough in the first instance by the mason, because it was customary to plaster over the whole surface when finishing the building.

This plastered face was whitewashed or treated with paintings, according to the funds available at the time or afterwards.

It must be remembered that these churches were fairly close to one another, as a rule, even in country districts, and I imagine that rivalry would sooner or later be the cause of many a plain church being painted.

In many cases to-day the plain walling inside the church is not plastered, but all the stones, which are fairly rough, are visible, showing the mortar joints— a condition of affairs often not mediaeval but due to some misguided restoration in which the ancient plastering was removed.

We must look for traces of colour and fragments of pictures and designs on all stonework, including vaulted roofs, on all timber roofs, on all stone and wood screens and fittings.

The predominant colour remaining to-day is, I should say, red, but this is probably due to the fact that this particular pigment is more lasting than the others, and we need not, I think, assume that it was originally the commonest. Some of the pictures however, may from the first have been in monochrome—that is, in one colour.

I give a few notes as to Period Characteristics.

SAXON.—Some very early examples have been found which would seem, from their position, to be of Saxon date. They are crude in drawing. The figures are badly proportioned in regard to the relative size of head and body.

NORMAN.—We must now expect development and improvement—for in later Norman times the ordinary painter had a serious rival in his brother-craftsmen who specialized in colour work in glass. We may look for a framework or pattern with forms that remind us of designs characteristic of the stone worker's methods, always slightly adapted to the different material, but the *motif* would often be the same.

EARLY ENGLISH.—Drawing still crude, but the result was very direct and definite, with no uncertainty as to its meaning.

There is a very well-thought-out picture of this period at Chaldon in Surrey. This example is very elaborate, considering the smallness of the church. It must have put the fear of God, in no uncertain way, into many a doubting Thomas. The main idea is this : A ladder—the Ladder of Life—is depicted, up which numerous souls are endeavouring, with more or less success, to climb, in order to reach Our Lord seated in glory above. In another part of the same picture Christ is shown advancing over the prostrate form of Satan. There are also shown, in a very lurid manner, the Tree of Life and the Torments of Hell. The final subject depicted is that of St. Michael, with scales, weighing the souls, and even here, in the presence of the saint, a demon is endeavouring to manipulate one side of the scales.

The people were reminded in this way, always upon entering or leaving their church, that any day, any moment, the quick and the dead might be called to judgment.

The sketch from East Bedfont (Fig. 145) shows another interesting example. On the left hand, Our Lord is depicted enthroned in majesty, with signs in hands and feet of the crucifixion, around are angels sounding trumpets and below are the dead rising from their graves. This represents the last day, the Day of Judgment, or Doom.

The colour decoration, apart from pictures, may be in the form of a pattern over the wall—as at

FIG. 145. REMAINS OF WALL PAINTING, EAST BEDFONT, MIDDLESEX

FIG. 146. REMAINS OF WALL PAINTING, HEXHAM. 1240 (?)

Hexham (Fig. 146)—following very much the period characteristics.

DECORATED AND PERPENDICULAR.—The work in these styles shows great advance and much elaboration. You will remember that the mouldings in this time were broader. This great breadth meant more scope for the painter with his colours. The woodwork also was more important than previously and more elaborate. This would lend itself well to colouring, and we must look to the elaborate wooden roofs and groined vaulting as well as to the numerous tombs and memorials for a very full treatment by colour.

STAINED AND PAINTED GLASS

In early Saxon times the windows were probably covered by horn, or some such substance in lieu of glass, through which the light would penetrate but not the rain. In many cases wooden shutters, which could be opened at will, were the only protection; examples have been found *in situ*. We know from remaining fragments, however, that there was plenty of stained glass in Norman times, not very much perhaps in the smaller churches, but certainly in the cathedrals.

Mediaeval glass was manufactured in small sheets of various colours, that is to say, colour was applied to the material when it was in a molten state. Most of these colours were mixed in the glass itself. These coloured pieces of glass were laid out and cut to form the required pattern. They were then painted with a brown stain where absolutely necessary, to give detail and shaded lines, such as the folds of a dress or the hair of a head.

After painting, these variously shaped pieces of glass were then put into the fire when all the added brown stain would become permanently burnt on. After removal from the fire the odd pieces of now coloured, painted, and burnt glass were sorted out and fixed in their proper places in a special lead framework, composed of long lengths of lead strips (themselves grooved to hold the edges of the glass), which strips were so twisted and turned that they formed part of the whole picture. One might form the boundary line to head or arm or hand as the case might be. The window was then ready for fixing into its stone framework in the building.

As this "leading" was chiefly used to form the pattern, the whole window, being made up of a great number of small pieces of glass each of one colour, produces an effect similar to mosaic (patterns of small pieces of stone and glass for floors and walls). The name "mosaic glass" particularly applies to the conventional patterns of small richly hued pieces as used in the Norman and Early English styles. In the Decorated and Perpendicular periods, however, a silver stain was used which gave a yellow tint where required to "white" glass, which was now fully utilized. "Abrasion" was also used, that is, red and blue (which were not used in the "pot metal"), and other colours were "flashed" on or applied as a layer to white glass. This layer could be removed where necessary to vary the design. Both these methods took away the "mosaic" effect and gave a much lighter character to glass of this period. Finally, in Tudor times, quite a different type of glass was used in which most of the design was painted on to the glass with less reliance on the leading and treated as a picture, and the term "painted glass" ought strictly to be applied to this distinct type of coloured glass.

What has already been said as to the damage suffered by wall paintings applies equally to coloured windows. But we must also bear in mind, in regard to the latter, that a good deal of alteration has often taken place in a window during its life. There is particular flexibility, and adaptability to repair, about the leadwork of these windows, so that it would be comparatively easy to make up one window out of the remains of two or three damaged ones. The picture will look a little mixed perhaps, but nevertheless this is the result we shall find to-day.

There exist fragments of what were once complete windows now distributed, forming parts of other windows scattered over various churches many miles apart. Fragments of glass now in French windows belong by right to English churches, and the reverse is just as true.

SUBJECTS.—Similar remarks to those already made in reference to the subjects for wall paintings may be applied to representations found depicted in glass. But I may add in the case of the latter that there is at times a portrait of the donor of the window or of a mediaeval king—or again some mediaeval bene-factor—either standing by itself or embodied in the treatment of a biblical subject.

1. NORMAN.—The glass was thick and uneven in colour. No white. Geometrical patterns in round and square panels.
2. EARLY ENGLISH.—All colours, but red was streaky. No white. Yellow was dull. Por-traits in panels. Pink or brown to represent flesh colour. Arranged in circular or quatre-

foil panels. Floral designs. Classic origin rather than in keeping with the contemporary Gothic. A canopy or roof formed over the subject as part of the design. The leadwork was strengthened by means of the addition of small iron bars. JESSE windows in the form of a genealogical tree.

3. DECORATED.—All colours and white. Yellow emphasized. Red clearer. Pale green sometimes for flesh tints. Trellis designs—natural leaves, fruit of vine, and ivy and oak, arranged as if growing on a trellis. Figures under canopies.

4. PERPENDICULAR.—Glass was thinner, except as when (as sometimes was the case) two coloured panes were superimposed when in a molten state. Less richness of colour. Plenty of yellow and white. Conventionalized, not natural, floral designs. Architectural designs. Figures, and canopies and pedestals. Donor represented in the picture. Stippling, that is, applying the paint with the brush end on, by means of short sharp dabs.

Modern research into the manner and matter of painted glass has not ended by simply satisfying the inquisitiveness of those who find interest and pleasure in studying old churches. It has also made possible the manufacture to-day of painted glass of similar quality and of the same satisfying beauty as that executed by mediaeval craftsmen. This is indeed a very satisfying truth. It could not have been said even a few years ago.

Bear in mind that much of the workmanship generally between the Perpendicular period and modern times has been of a decadent nature, and we

may well be proud to belong to a time when the age
of revival may be said to have dawned.

From Norman times down to the most recent war-
memorial painted glass window there has been a continuous story, but by no means a progressive one, as
regards quality.

Let us see that the work of to-day be worthy of
the modern sacrifices which surely vie with those of
our ancestors; let us encourage our modern artists
and craftsmen, who are once again able and willing
to produce work equal to the high standard which
prevailed in mediaeval times.

FIG. 146A.   LEADED BORDER AND " MOSAIC " GLASS IN GEOMETRICAL PATTERNS
WITH PAINTED FOLIAGE (EARLY ENGLISH)

CHAPTER XIV

BRASSES

MEMORIALS to the dead crowd our village churches. They are always of great interest, and are, at the same time, often of considerable beauty, especially when they are not only inscribed with names and dates, but follow in their design the usual characteristics of the period in which they were made. The earlier memorials are of floor slabs, which later were usually covered with brasses or figured sheets of brass. Later, these slabs were raised above the floor, forming "table tombs," which in turn grew into veritable monuments which in many instances had columns supporting miniature roofs and canopies all richly moulded and carved; and so arranged and designed that you will at once be able on inspecting any example to say that it belongs to a particular period, as in the reference made when we were dealing with the Decorated Period (Fig. 108).

The mediaeval habit of dating these monuments is both interesting and important, for until now I have been dealing with certain forms of the main structure, which are never dated, and we can only know by study and experience the date of their erection. True, we may occasionally find a dated stone in a wall which suggests the year in which that wall was built, but there is never any proof that a clever mason, probably of post-mediaeval date, did not, when building or rebuilding the wall, take this particular stone from a near-by ruin and build it into the newer wall. When, however, on the other hand, we find a monument with the date carved thereon as part of its design, we may surely feel that we have some definite proof as to when the monument was constructed.

So we meet, for example, with a beautifully executed memorial of such design that we judge from our experience that it is of, say, the Decorated period ; then, looking for a date, are not surprised to see that it is within a few years of the year 1300.

BRASSES.—Memorials covered with brass form a distinct class, and you will find ample opportunity to study " Brasses " as they are called. They are very common here in our parish churches, compared with their use on the Continent. The subject is, however, far too large for justice to be done to it here, but there are several textbooks which deal solely with them, as quoted at the end of this book. These books and the brasses themselves will prove, I am sure, a fascinating study, and one in which some will wish to specialize, as in other subjects such as paintings, after mastering the general outline of mediaeval architecture.

A brass is a thin, flat, incised sheet of metal let into a corresponding sinking on a stone background known as a MATRIX. The incisions on the plate may represent in picture form either some cleric, knight, lady, civilian, or even a skeleton.

The only place in a church in which to look with any certainty for a date is on a brass. This dating of brasses is of the greatest interest, for here we shall find examples of contemporary armour and dress exactly as worn in definite times in the past.

I will ask you to protest with me, when opportunities occur, against the modern practice of taking

L

up old brasses from the floor, where they were originally laid in their natural position, and putting them on to a wall. The comparatively thin plate of brass was intended to lie in a horizontal position on the floor or on a tomb, not to be fixed upright against a wall as if it were a hanging tapestry.

Where a monument was required on or against a wall it is of stone, or other suitable material. The foot traffic over the brass on the floor has only a slight deteriorating effect on the particularly hard alloy or " latten " of which it is made, but it is easy to rope off the space or cover the brass in some way. Placing it on the wall where the atmospheric conditions vary more than at the floor level is not preserving the brass. It is merely a question of suitability of material to place. Only quite a small brass can be said to be properly placed when fixed to a wall.

PALIMPSEST BRASSES.—Each individual brass may have had its history, much as we found in the case of painted windows. A brass may have been stolen, or have been discarded, laid by for a while, and then engraved on the reverse side, and used again as a new memorial. Some of the examples, therefore, that we see to-day have older engravings on their backs. Sometimes the same side of a brass was adapted with slight alterations. All are called PALIMPSEST (or re-used) BRASSES.

Speaking generally on this subject, the following notes may be of some guide as to the period.

EARLY ENGLISH.—There are no known examples of this period, but there is a matrix (stone) at St. Paul's, Bedford, of this time, believed to date about 1208, the brass from which is missing.

DECORATED AND PERPENDICULAR. EDWARD I and EDWARD II (1272–1327).—Few brasses. The knights are shown in chain mail (early) or plate armour (late). Head shown on helmet (knight) or on cushion. Hair curly. The legs crossed or not (of no significance). Feet *against* lion (knight), hound (civilian), lapdog (lady). Ladies have loose-fitting mantles. Mostly life size. Some have canopies. Border inscriptions.

EDWARD III and RICHARD II (1327–1399).—The brasses at Cobham in Kent and Stoke D'Abernon in Surrey should be studied. Ladies with close-fitting dress with loose mantle over. Some canopies. Border inscription and inscription at foot.

LANCASTRIAN (1406–1453).—Many examples. Deterioration. This form of memorial popular with all classes including wool merchants and judges. Many variations. Some bracket brasses. Not always inscriptions at foot ; sometimes also on border.

YORKIST (1453–1485).—The ladies were shown with a BUTTERFLY head-dress. This is a wire framework covered with material which was made thereby to stand out from the head. For this reason the head was shown in profile. The attitude of the men's heads followed suit. Feet on, not against, the ground. Fewer canopies. Smaller brasses.

To quote from Mr. J. S. M. Ward's book : " During the Wars of the Roses, the Knights usually charged on horseback. This explains why the heavier armour is on the upper part of the body, whilst the lower is more lightly protected. Often, therefore, the upper half seems out of proportion."

M

BOOKS TO READ

GENERAL

"The English Parish Church." Cox. (Batsford.)

"A.B.C. of Gothic Architecture." Parker. (Oxford.)

"A Concise Glossary of Architecture." (Parker.)

"A History of Architecture." Fletcher. 7th edition. (Batsford.)

"Gothic Architecture in England." Bond. (Batsford.)

"The Historical Growth of the English Parish Church." Thompson. (Univ. Press, Cambridge.)

The "Little Guides" Series. (Methuen.)

SAXON ARCHITECTURE: "Arts in Early England." Baldwin Brown.

PAINTED GLASS: "Ancient, Stained, and Painted Glass." F. S. Eden. (Univ. Press, Cambridge.)

"Brasses." J. S. M. Ward. (Univ. Press, Cambridge.)

BUILDINGS TO SEE

LONDON

Norman

Tower of London.
St. Bartholomew's, Smithfield.
St. John's, Clerkenwell (Crypt).
Bow Church (Crypt).

Transition

Temple Church (nave).

Early English

Public Record Office (arch in Courtyard).
St. Saviour's, Southwark.
Westminster Abbey.

Decorated

St. Mary Undercroft (Crypt), Westminster Hall.
St. Ethelburga's, Bishopsgate.
St. Etheldreda's, Ely Place, Holborn.
The Dutch Church, Austin Friars.

Perpendicular

St. Helen's, Bishopsgate.
St. Olave's, Hart Street.

Specimens of all periods

Victoria and Albert Museum.

PROVINCES

See "The Little Guides" Series (Methuen).

INDEX

NOTE.—All numbers refer to pages; those shown in heavy type refer to pages upon which illustrations occur.

PRINTED BY
JARROLD AND SONS LTD,
NORWICH